Scotts Bluff

Scotts Bluff National Monument, Nebraska
Text by Merrill J. Mattes

National Park Service
U.S. Department of the Interior
Washington, DC 1958 (revised 1992)

Contents

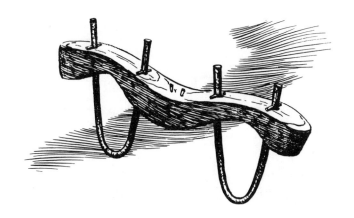

S COTTS BLUFF *was a celebrated landmark on the great North Platte Valley trunkline of "the Oregon Trail," the traditional route of over-land migration to Oregon, California, and Utah. Today the massive castellated bluff looks down upon concrete highways, railways, airports, irri-gated farms, and bustling communities of the mid-20th century; but it is the same awe-inspiring sentinel which 100 years ago watched the passage of countless trains of ox-drawn covered wagons, and the twinkling of many campfires. Scotts Bluff National Monument keeps alive the epic story of our ancestors who dared cross the wilderness of plains and mountains to plant the western stars in the American flag.*

Present Scotts Bluff is but a part of the historic "Scott's Bluffs" named for Hiram Scott, an employee of the Rocky Mountain Fur Company, whose skeleton was found in the vicinity in 1829. The first known published reference is to be found in *The Adventures of Captain Bonne-ville,* by Washington Irving, published in 1837. The first map to show this landmark is in Robert Greenhow's *Memoir, Historical and Political on the Northwest Coast of North America,* published in 1840. It appeared next in the Fremont map of 1843, which became basic for later emigrant guides.

Early Exploration of the Great Plains

In 1540 the Spaniard Coronado captained a treasure-hunting expedi-tion from Mexico across Arizona, New Mexico, and the Texas Pan-handle. From there he led a picked detachment of armored horsemen

---

Scotts Bluff visitor center. Courtesy Christian Studio, Gering, Nebr.

Returning Astorians at Scotts Bluff Christmas Day, 1812.

to mythical *Quivira*, which proved to be only a squalid Indian village in central Kansas. Contrary to long-held belief, Coronado never reached present Nebraska. The first Spaniards known to have penetrated this state—an exploring party of 1720 led by Pedro de Villasur—were massacred by Pawnees at the forks of the Platte.

Following LaSalle's traverse of the Mississippi and the establishment of French settlements along that river, several French explorers—notably Bourgmont and Charlevois—penetrated the fringe of the Great Plains, bringing back reports of strange shaggy beasts in numbers so vast that they blackened the landscape. The Platte River was named by Frenchmen who explored its lower reaches; for this is the French word for "flat," a literal translation of the Oto word, "Nebrathka." The Upper Platte was not explored by Frenchmen until 1739 when the Mallet brothers lead a small party from the mouth of the Niobrara across Nebraska, up the South Platte, and thence to Santa Fe. The high tide of French exploration of the Plains was marked in 1743 by the long journey, on foot, of the Verendrye brothers from the Missouri River westward. How far west they traveled has been a widely debated subject, but most scholars believe that they reached the vicinity of the Black Hills of South Dakota.

The famous Lewis and Clark Expedition of 1804-6, dispatched by President Jefferson to explore the newly acquired Louisiana Territory, followed the natural passageway of the upper Missouri and Columbia Rivers to become the first Americans to cross the continent. While they triumphantly returned to St. Louis, Lt. Zebulon Pike visited a Pawnee village on the Upper Republican River, then proceeded southwestward up the Arkansas. In the wake of these official explorers came the fur trappers and traders, a strange breed of men who traced out and rough-mapped the tributary streams of the western plains and mountains in their search for beaver hides. The early history of Scotts Bluff is closely linked with the history of the western American fur trade.

First White Men at Scotts Bluff

Fur traders were the first white men known to have seen Scotts Bluff. They were the returning Astorians—a group of seven men under Robert Stuart, traveling from their trading post at the mouth of the Columbia River to St. Louis. On Christmas day, 1812, Stuart recorded in his journal:

> 21 miles same course brought us to camp in the bare Prairie, but were fortunate in finding enough of driftwood for our culinary purpose. The Hills on the south have lately approached the river, are remarkably rugged and Bluffy and possess a few Cedars. Buffaloe very few in numbers and mostly Bulls.

The Astorian Expedition of 1811, so-called because it was an enterprise of the wealthy fur trader, John Jacob Astor, comprised the second group of Americans to span the continent. Led by Wilson Price Hunt, the "Astorians" ascended the Missouri River until they were blocked by the treacherous Arikara or "Ree" Indians near the mouth of Grand River. Then they traveled overland, skirting the Black Hills and the Bighorn Mountains, and reached their Columbia River headwaters via Jackson Hole. Joining forces with another Astor group who had reached the mouth of the Columbia by ship, they built Astoria, the first American trading post on the Pacific slope. In 1812, Robert Stuart and his small band started back overland to carry messages to Astor. By their successful mission they performed one of the great feats of western exploration, for in their perilous journey eastward they blazed the route via the Upper Snake, Green, and North Platte Rivers which was destined to become the Oregon Trail! (See map on pages 30, 31.)

Constantly imperiled by exposure, starvation, and Indians, they crossed the Continental Divide near South Pass and descended the Sweetwater and North Platte Rivers. After they had passed Scotts Bluff, the hostility of the wintry Plains impelled them to retrace their steps to a point near present Torrington, Wyo., where they camped for the winter and built canoes. Early in the spring of 1813 they resumed their journey. They were unable to navigate the shallow, braided, upper reaches of the Platte River, and it was not until they reached Grand Island, that they successfully launched their canoes.

Rediscovery of the Central Overland Route

Stuart's journal was not published until many years later, and the tremendous import of his geographical discovery—a central route across the continent—was lost amid preoccupation with the War of 1812 and the seizure of Astoria by the British forces. For the next decade the fur traders, operating out of St. Louis, concentrated on sending expeditions up the Missouri River, persisting in their notion that this was the only logical route westward. Manual Lisa, William Ashley, Andrew Henry, and Joshua Pilcher were among the leaders of numerous invasions of the Upper Missouri country. Beaver pelts were plentiful, but the Blackfoot, Ree, Gros Ventre, and other Indian tribes were unfriendly. A series of disastrous encounters with these Indians reached a crisis in 1823, when a large fur brigade under William Ashley was treacherously attacked above Grand River by the Rees, the same who had blocked the path of the Astorians 11 years before. An appeal for military aid resulted in an expedition from Fort Atkinson (above present Omaha) under Col. Henry Leavenworth. The Indian villages were besieged but the results were indecisive. Thereupon Ashley and his men abandoned their efforts on the Upper Missouri, and struck out overland to the mountains. This decision led to the discovery of the rich beaver valleys of the central Rockies, and the rediscovery of South Pass and the Great Platte route. It ushered in the historic Rocky Mountain fur trade, and opened a new chapter in the history of Scotts Bluff.

Among the enterprising young men employed by Ashley, who received their baptism of fire at the Ree villages, were several destined to achieve great fame in the annals of the West. Conspicuous among them were Jim Bridger and Etienne Provost, who soon discovered the Great Salt Lake; Jedediah Smith, who led a band of trappers across

Ree Indian attack on General Ashley's trappers.

the Black Hills and the Bighorn Mountains to explore the headwaters of the Green and Snake Rivers, and to become the first American to challenge the supremacy of British fur traders in the Oregon country; William Sublette, who became the founder of Fort William on the Laramie River; Thomas Fitzpatrick, noted "mountain man," emigrant guide, and Indian agent; and Hiram Scott, one of Ashley's clerks who would soon die tragically near the bluff which now bears his name.

If any white men traveled by Scotts Bluff in the decade following the downstream passage of the returning Astorians, they left no distinct record. It is surmised that Canadian half-breeds roamed and trapped in this region during this period since several geographic names of French origin seem to have survived from the earliest days of the fur trade. Laramie or "La Ramee" River and Goshen or "Goche's" Hole, both in nearby Wyoming, tell of early trappers about whom there survive only the haziest traditions. We can only say that the second group of white men in the North Platte Valley who can be positively identified were four of Ashley's trappers who, in the spring of 1824, attempted to bring their beaver pelts down the Platte River. With this event, Scotts Bluff once more emerges on the pages of history.

Following a successful harvest of beaver, Jedediah Smith delegated Thomas Fitzpatrick, James Clyman, and two others to transport the pelts to Fort Atkinson. This led directly to the rediscovery of the strategic Platte route and the beginning of a half century during which Scotts Bluff became one of the great landmarks of that historic route. Fitzpatrick failed in his effort to transport the furs down the Sweet-water by bullboat (Indian boat made from buffalo hides stretched over a frame of green willow boughs) and, lacking horses, was compelled to cache them near Independence Rock. He and his companions were subsequently scattered by marauding Indians, but they all arrived safely at Fort Atkinson. Fitzpatrick promptly took horses back to Independence Rock to retrieve his furs, and so passed Scotts Bluff three times in 1824.

The Rocky Mountain Fur Trade

Ashley was impressed by Fitzpatrick's report on the success of his employees in locating rich beaver territory. Late in the autumn of 1824, he hurried westward up the Platte River, sending his brigades out to trap while he personally led an exploration of the lower canyons of

Annual rendezvous of Rocky Mountain trappers.

the Green River. In 1825, reunited with his men at Henry's Fork of the Green, he led them to the head of Wind River where they constructed boats and floated their cargo to St. Louis via the Bighorn, Yellowstone, and Missouri Rivers.

Ashley is credited with conceiving a new scheme of handling the mountain fur trade which became known as the rendezvous system. Instead of building expensive fixed trading posts in the wilderness, dependent upon the Indian trade, the idea was to send white trappers to camp out all winter, trapping while the beaver were in prime fur, then all to foregather at some prearranged mountain valley where they would meet traders bringing pack trains of equipment and trade goods from St. Louis. Casks of whisky, standard trade items, insured that the annual mountain carnival or rendezvous would see not only a rapid exchange of trade goods for beaver pelts, but also carousing and roistering on a scale suitable to compensate the trappers for their long lonely winter vigils. For 15 years Scotts Bluff would witness traders' caravans, going mountainward in early summer, and returning in the autumn laden with their harvest of furs.

In the summer of 1826 the first of the colorful traders' caravans, led by Ashley, Sublette, and Smith, and probably including young Hiram Scott, passed the yet unnamed bluff en route to the first big rendezvous, on the shores of the Great Salt Lake in Utah. The swarthy, colorfully garbed trappers escorted 300 pack-laden mules on this trip. At Salt Lake there were two notable events. Ashley, who had now become comfortably rich from skimming the cream of the beaver trade, sold his interests to a partnership which became known as the Rocky Mountain Fur Company, and Smith embarked on the first of his notable expeditions across the Great Basin to California, becoming the first American to reach that Mexican province by this route.

The Tragedy of Scotts Bluff

The year 1827 went much as those before, with another rendezvous at Salt Lake where Smith reported his adventures. He then set off on another California trip (followed by a side trip up the Pacific Coast to Oregon, where most of his men were massacred by Indians on the Umpquah). Hiram Scott was among the traders who returned that year to St. Louis. This we know from a document dated October 16, 1827, preserved in the files of the Missouri Historical Society, for Scott is there listed as an employee of Ashley (who continued to operate the supply train), having earned $280 in wages for his season's labor.

That Scott ranked high in the esteem of the fur trading fraternity is attested not only by this document but also by the official records of the Leavenworth Expedition of 1823, wherein Scott shares with Jedediah Smith the distinction of being a "captain of volunteers" under General Ashley.   In another document, a letter of April 11, 1827, written by Ashley at Lexington, Mo., Scott is described as "alive to our interest" and "properly efficient."   One other source implies that he was a trader of high rank.   These meager facts are all we know about Hiram Scott, who was doomed to die mysteriously a year later, while returning with the homeward-bound caravan of the Rocky Mountain Fur Company.

The facts concerning Hiram Scott's death are even scarcer than those about his career.   There is a wealth of tradition and legend, but these cannot be accepted as established facts.   Of the innumerable versions, almost no two are identical.

The classic account of Scott's death, and the one first published (in 1837), is that given in Washington Irving's story of the adventures of Capt. Benjamin Bonneville, on leave from the United States Army. Irving relates that on June 21, 1832, the Bonneville party

> . . . encamped amid high and beetling cliffs of indurated clay and sand-stone, bearing the semblance of towers, castles, churches and fortified cities.   At a distance it was scarcely possible to persuade one's self that the works of art were not mingled with these fantastic freaks of nature. They have received the name of Scott's Bluffs from a melancholy circumstance.   A number of years since, a party were descending the upper part of the river in canoes, when their frail barks were overturned and all their powder spoiled.   Their rifles being thus rendered useless, they were unable to procure food by hunting and had to depend upon roots and wild fruits for subsistence.   After suffering extremely from hunger, they arrived at Laramie's Fork, a small tributary of the north branch of the Nebraska, about sixty miles above the cliffs just mentioned.   Here one of the party, by the name of Scott, was taken ill; and his companions came to a halt, until he should recover health and strength sufficient to proceed.   While they were searching round in quest of edible roots they discovered a fresh trail of white men, who had evidently but recently preceded them.   What was to be done?   By a forced march they might overtake this party, and thus be able to reach the settlements in safety. Should they linger they might all perish of famine and exhaustion.   Scott, however, was incapable of moving; they were too feeble to aid him forward, and dreaded that such a clog would prevent their coming up with the advance party.   They determined, therefore, to abandon him to his fate.   Accordingly, under pretence of seeking food, and such simples as might be efficacious in his malady, they deserted him and hastened forward upon the trail.   They succeeded in overtaking the party of which they were in quest, but concealed their faithless desertion of Scott; alleging that he had died of disease.
>
> On the ensuing summer, these very individuals visiting these parts in company with others, came suddenly upon the bleached bones and grinning skull of a human skeleton, which by certain signs they recognized for the remains of Scott.   This was sixty long miles from the place where they had abandoned him; and it appeared that the wretched man had crawled that immense distance before death put an end to his miseries. The wild and picturesque bluffs in the neighborhood of his lonely grave have ever since borne his name.

Trappers skinning beaver.

A very touching and pathetic story, but it is quite different from the version offered by Warren Ferris of the American Fur Company. In 1830, he passed Scotts Bluff on the north side of the river 2 years ahead of Captain Bonneville, and just 2 years after the event:

We encamped opposite to "Scott's Bluffs," so called in respect to the memory of a young man who was left here alone to die a few years previous. He was a clerk in a company returning from the mountains, the leader of which found it necessary to leave him behind at a place some distance above this point, in consequence of a severe illness which rendered him unable to ride. He was consequently placed in a bullhide boat, in charge of two men, who had orders to convey him by water down to these bluffs, where the leader of the party promised to await their coming. After a weary and hazardous voyage, they reached the appointed rendezvous, and found to their surprise and bitter disappointment, that the company had continued on down the river without stopping for them to overtake and join it.

Left thus in the heart of a wide wilderness, hundreds of miles from any point where assistance or succour could be obtained, and surrounded by predatory bands of savages thirsting for blood and plunder, could any condition be deemed more hopeless or deplorable? They had, moreover, in descending the river, met with some accident, either the loss of the means of procuring subsistence or defending their lives in case of discovery and attack. This unhappy circumstance, added to the fact that the river was filled with innumerable shoals and sand-bars, by which its navigation was rendered almost impracticable, determined them to forsake their charge and boat together, and push on night and day until they should overtake the company, which they did on the second or third day afterward.

The reason given by the leader of the company for not fulfilling his promise, was that his men were starving, no game could be found, and he was compelled to proceed in quest of buffalo.

Poor Scott! We will not attempt to picture what his thoughts must have been after his cruel abandonment, nor harrow up the feelings of the reader, by a recital of what agonies he must have suffered before death put an end to his misery.

The bones of a human being were found the spring following, on the opposite side of the river, which were supposed to be the remains of Scott. It was conjectured that in the energy of despair, he had found strength to carry him across the stream, and then had staggered about the prairie, till God in pity took him to Himself.

Such are the sad chances to which the life of the Rocky Mountain adventurer is exposed.

The Hiram Scott legend is mentioned by almost all early travelers who have left record of a journey up the North Platte Valley, but it would be fruitless to recite the many other varied, conflicting, and often quaint versions of how he died. There are differences of opinion as to the distance the poor fellow crawled, if any; whether the party traveled on foot or by horseback, muleback, bullboat, raft, or canoe; whether he was a victim of Indians, exposure, drowning, freezing, disease, or starvation; the location of his skeleton; the identity and number of his companions; whether their desertion was premeditated; whether it was justified; how their treachery was exposed; and, finally, whether the whole thing might not have been a grisly hoax!

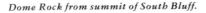

Dome Rock from summit of South Bluff.

It was not a hoax. Though the legend has become hopelessly confused, research has proved that there was a Hiram Scott prominent in the Rocky Mountain fur trade from 1823 until 1827; and that he disappeared in 1828 and was never heard from thereafter, except through the faint echoes of the legend. His companions remain unidentified, but research strongly suggests that William Sublette was the leader of the 1828 caravan, who issued instructions to these men to remain with him; and it was William Sublette who led the springtime caravan of 1829 that discovered Scott's skeleton, miles away from the spot where they reported he had died.

Rufus B. Sage, who passed the bluff in 1841, was particularly impressed with the melancholy circumstances of Scott's death, and was moved to impassioned poetry:

No willing grave received the corpse
of this poor lonely one; —
His bones, alas, were left to bleach
and moulder 'neath the sun!

The night-wolf howl'd his requiem, —
the rude winds danced his dirge;
And e'er anon, in mournful chime
sigh's forth the mellow surge!

The spring shall teach the rising grass
to twine for him a tomb;
And, o'er the spot where he doth lie,
shall bid the wild flowers bloom.

But, far from friends, and far from home,
ah, dismal thought, to die!
Ah, let me 'mid my friends expire,
and with my fathers lie.

The mountain men have engraved their names on the topography of the West with such place names as Scotts Bluff, Jackson Hole, Colter Bay, Bridger Pass, Sublette County, Provo, Ogden, and Carson City which forever remind us of these colorful figures with seven-league boots who spearheaded the invasion of the West.

The First Wagons

In 1827 Ashley had sent a wheeled cannon up the Platte route to impress the Indians at Great Salt Lake. However, the first bona fide wagons on the Oregon Trail were those of the Smith-Jackson-Sublette caravan of 1830, headed for the rendezvous scheduled in the Wind River Valley, near present Lander. In a famous letter to Secretary of War Eaton, the partners reported a caravan of ten wagons, drawn by five mules each, and two dearborns, drawn by one mule each . . . eighty-one men in company, all mounted on mules. . . .

For our support, at leaving the Missouri settlements, until we should get into the buffalo country, we drove twelve head of cattle, beside a milk cow . . . . We began to fall in with the buffaloes on the Platte, about three hundred and fifty miles from the white settlements; and from that time lived on buffaloes, the quantity being infinitely beyond what we needed. . . . The country being almost all open, level, and prairie, the chief obstructions were ravines and creeks, the banks of which required cutting down, and for this purpose a few pioneers were generally kept ahead of the caravan. This is the first time that wagons ever went to the Rocky mountains; and the ease and safety with which it was done prove the facility of communicating over land with the Pacific ocean.

At Wind River the parties sold their interest to another group of seasoned trappers — Fitzpatrick, Bridger, Fraeb, Gervais, and Milton Sublette. Thus far the Rocky Mountain Fur Company had a monopoly of the choice beaver country, except for occasional brushes with the Hudson's Bay Company in the Snake River country. Now an ominous rival presented itself, Astor's powerful American Fur Company, which sought to regain the trading empire lost during the War of 1812. In a brief time Astor's company would outmaneuver the Rocky Mountain Fur Company, absorb its leaders, and take over the monopoly. But first there would be fierce competition. In the vanguard of this invasion came a pack train headed by Joseph Robidoux and William Vanderburgh. They passed Scotts Bluff on May 27, on the north side of the river, just a few days behind their rivals. Robidoux and Vanderburgh's adventures have been chronicled by Warren Ferris.

Hiram Scott was not the only casualty in this dangerous fur trading. Jedediah Smith was slain by Comanches in 1831 on the Cimarron River, en route to Santa Fe. Vanderburgh was soon killed by Blackfeet Indians near the Three Forks of the Missouri. Kit Carson later killed a fellow trapper in a duel over an Arapahoe maiden on the Upper Hoback River, and Thomas Fitzpatrick suffered serious injuries from a near-fatal encounter with the Gros Ventres. The mortality rate among the mountain men was high, but the survivors continued their annual rendezvous. The decade of the 1830's was the golden age of the fur trade.

Captain Bonneville, who launched the Hiram Scott legend, made history in 1832 by taking his loaded wagons across the Continental Divide at South Pass, foreshadowing the mighty covered wagon migration that would begin within a decade. While Bonneville built a fort on the Upper Green, the rendezvous of 1832 was held in Pierre's Hole, on the west slope of the Tetons, and here the assembled trappers had a famous pitched battle with the Gros Ventres, which resulted in several fatalities.

Smith-Jackson-Sublette Expedition of 1830.
Sketch by William H. Jackson.

Among those in Sublette's train in 1833 was Sir William Drummond Stewart of Scotland, a wealthy adventurer, the first of a series of notable Britishers to travel through the West, recording their impressions. We are indebted to him, as well as to Warren Ferris, Osborne Russell, and Joe Meek for vivid pictures of the wild and colorful rendezvous scenes. From 1833 until 1840, these rendezvous were held on the Upper Green, near present Daniel, Wyo.

Traders, Missionaries, and Adventurers

The year 1834 was a lively one along the trappers' trail up the North Platte. This was the year that Robert Campbell and William Sublette halted their caravan at the mouth of Laramie's Fork, some 60 miles above Scotts Bluff, to establish log-palisaded Fort William, the first of a succession of trading posts, and later a military post, which became the great way-station on the Oregon Trail, called Fort Laramie. A few days behind Sublette, Nathaniel Wyeth led a caravan upriver to establish rival Fort Hall in Idaho. With Wyeth were Thomas Nuttall and John Townsend, the first men of scientific attainments to follow the trail, and Jason and Daniel Lee, first Methodist missionaries to Oregon.

The earliest known sketch of Scotts Bluff, 1837. Courtesy, Enron Art Foundation/Joslyn Art Museum, Omaha, Nebr. Sketch by Alfred J. Miller.

14

In 1835, when the American Fur Company emerged as the dominant trading concern, it took over Fort William on the Laramie and placed Lucien Fontenelle in charge there. That year Presbyterian missionaries Samuel Parker and Marcus Whitman accompanied Fontenelle and the traders' caravan to the rendezvous on the Green River, then went on to scout the Oregon country.

Impressed by what he saw, Marcus Whitman quickly returned to the States to organize more missionaries. In 1836 he brought his wife, Narcissa, and the Rev. Henry Spalding and his wife, Elizabeth, westward to Oregon. These two white women, the first ever to see Scotts Bluff and the first to reach Oregon, were well guarded on their journey by the veteran Thomas Fitzpatrick and his swarthy crew.

At Scotts Bluff the Whitman party met company employees from Fort Laramie, descending the Platte River in fur-laden bullboats. This was to become a common method of transporting furs to St. Louis, although the shallow Platte was poorly suited to navigation, and the boats often came to grief on sandbars. The trips could only be made during the June rise of the Platte. Since travelers from the States usually arrived at Scotts Bluff by mid-June, the trappers' boats were often reported in this vicinity.

It was in 1837 that Scotts Bluff, the martial sentinel of the North Platte Valley, stood for its first portrait. The magnificent sketch, now preserved in the Walters Art Gallery in Baltimore, was the work of Alfred J. Miller, a talented artist who accompanied Sir William Drummond Stewart and William Sublette to the Green River rendezvous. Miller's notes on Scotts Bluff reflect the same awe and imagination that inspired countless later emigrants. He writes, "At a distance as we approached it the appearance was that of an immense fortification with bastions, towers, battlements, embrazures, scarps and counterscarps." He records also that this neighborhood abounded in delicious "Rocky Mountain pheasant," and in jack rabbits, antelope, and bighorn.

The supply train of 1838, led by Andrew Drips, was accompanied by another missionary party, including the journalist Myra F. Eells, who commented on the "grand scenery" of the bluffs, and the Swiss fortune hunter, August Johann Sutter, on whose California ranch the discovery of gold 10 years later would precipitate the most famous migration in American history.

In 1839, Dr. Frederick Wislizenus from St. Louis, traveling to Fort Laramie with the caravan led by Moses Harris, described the bluff:

... We traveled somewhat away from the river, toward the left, and enjoyed a picturesque landscape. All about were rocks piled up by Nature in merry mood, giving full scope to fancy in the variety of their shapes. Some were perfect cones; others flat round tops; others, owing to their crenulated projections, resembled fortresses; others old castles, porticos, etc. Most of them were sparsely covered with pine and cedar. The scenery has obvious resemblance to several places in Saxon Switzerland.

The last of the traditional rendezvous was held in 1840 on the Green River. This year's expedition was led by Andrew Drips, and it was made notable by two parties who accompanied it. One was the Joel Walker family, the first avowed Oregon emigrants; the others were Jesuit priests headed by Father Pierre-Jean De Smet, who would become one of the West's most prodigious travelers and reporters. Like many others, De Smet, impressed by the scenery of the North Platte, wrote:

> . . . In the neighborhood of this wonder [Chimney Rock], all the hills present a singular aspect; some have the appearance of towers, castles and fortified cities. From a little distance, one can hardly persuade himself that art is not mingled in them with the fantasies of nature. Bands of the *ashata,* an animal called also *grosse-corne,* or bighorn, have their abode in the midst of these bad lands. . . . [Scotts Bluff], with its castles and fantastic cities, forms the termination of a high ridge, which runs from south to north. We found a narrow passage through between two perpendicular cliffs 300 feet in height [Mitchell Pass].

Migration to Oregon

The era of the transcontinental covered wagon migrations began in 1841, for in that year came the initial band of 80 Oregon homeseekers, guided by Thomas Fitzpatrick and accompanied by Father De Smet on his second western journey. John Bidwell was the historian of this expedition. Another traveler was Joseph Williams, an elderly but energetic Methodist preacher, who described the building of Fort John (the second Fort Laramie). Although the beaver trade had declined, a brisk trade with the Indians for buffalo robes continued, and the American Fur Company would occupy Laramie's Fork for eight more years.

Dr. Elijah White, the new agent for the Oregon Indians, lead a party of 112 westward in 1842. Among them was Medorem Crawford, who described Scotts Bluff as "the most romantic scenery I ever saw." Lansford W. Hastings, who was to write one of the first emigrant guidebooks, was also of this party. Lt. John C. Fremont's first expedition to the Rocky Mountains traveled up the Platte in 1842; his official report would likewise become a standard reference. He described Scotts Bluff as "an escarpment on the river of about 900 yards in length" which "forces the road to make a considerable circuit over the uplands." He found the plain between the bluffs and

Original road bed of the Oregon Trail at Scotts Bluff.

Chimney Rock almost entirely covered with driftwood, testifying to a recent flood.

In 1843 Scotts Bluff witnessed the first mass migration to Oregon; it was promoted by Marcus Whitman. In May more than 1,000 persons, including 130 women and 610 children, left Independence, Mo., for the long trek overland. This well-organized expedition, with military rules to ensure protection, an elected captain, and division into companies, set the pattern for the hundreds of emigrant trains to follow. The elected captain was Peter Burnett who was to become the first Governor of California in 1850. The "Cow Column," the last and slowest of the 1843 companies, has achieved fame through the writings of Jesse Applegate. Overton Johnson relates that the train reached camp "by a fine Spring, at the foot of Scott's Bluffs" on July 9.

Close behind the emigrant families came an elaborate hunting party, led by Sir William Stewart and William Sublette, making their farewell visit to the mountains. Baptiste Charbonneau, the infant son who had been carried by Sacajawea on the Lewis and Clark Expedition, was hired as a driver. William Clark Kennerly's reminiscences of this journey tells of a frightening incident that occurred near Scotts Bluff:

Far out on the Platte one morning, while making preparations for our daily hunt, we descried coming toward us a herd, which I can state without any exageration must have numbered a million. The pounding of their hooves on the hard prairie sounded like the roaring of a mighty ocean, surging over the land and sweeping everything before it. Here was more game than we bargained for, and the predicament in which we now found ourselves gave us much cause for alarm. On they came, and as we were directly in their path and on the bank of the river, there was great danger of our being swept over. This danger was averted only by our exerting every effort to turn them off in another direction; and as it took the herd two entire days to pass, even at quite a rapid gait, we were kept busy placing guards of shouting, gesticulating men in the daytime and building huge bonfires at night.

In the summer of 1844 four emigrant trains passed Scotts Bluff bound for Oregon. One of these was piloted by James Clyman, who had first seen the bluff 20 years before on his long hike from Independence Rock to Fort Atkinson. In his diary Clyman wrote:

. . . encamped in the midtst of Scotts blufs By a cool spring in a romantic & picturisque vally surounded except to the E. by high & allmost impassably steep clay cliffs of all immagenary shapes & forms supped on a most dlecious piece of venison from the loin of a fat Black taild Buck and I must not omit to mention that I took my rifle and (and) walked out in the deep ravin to guard a Beautifull covey of young Ladies & misses while they gathered wild currants & choke chirries which grow in great perfusion in this region and of the finerst kind.

The trek to Oregon in 1845 dwarfed all that had gone before. An informal count at Fort Laramie revealed that 5,000 people and 500 ox-drawn wagons were on the march. The charms of Scotts Bluff, and the tragic tale of its namesake, were not lost on the many diarists, among them Joel Palmer, who credits "Scott's Bluffs" with a good spring and an abundance of wood and grass. Below the bluffs, says Palmer,

We met a company of mountaineers from Fort Laramie, who had started for the settlements early in the season, with flat-boats loaded with buffalo robes, and other articles of Indian traffic. The river became so low, that they were obliged to lay by; part of the company had returned to the fort for teams; others were at the boat landing, while fifteen of the party were footing their way to the States. They were a jolly set of fellows. . . .

In this same big year the United States Government sent its first military expedition up the Platte. Guided by Fitzpatrick, Col. S. W. Kearny led five companies of the First Dragoons to South Pass. A few days ahead of the Oregon Trek, on June 11 they encamped "below Scotts Bluffs, and directly opposite a large village of Dacotah [Sioux] Indians."

Emigrants fording the Platte. River crossings were a dangerous obstacle to prairie schooners.

. . . that immense and celebrated pile, called "Scott's Bluffs," advances across the plain nearly to the water's edge. If one could increase the size of the Alhambra of Grenada, or the Castle of Heidelberg, which Professor Longfellow has so poetically and so graphically described,—twenty fold in every way but in height,—he could form some idea of the magnitude and splendor of this chef d'oeuvre of Nature at Palace-Building.

Years of Decision, 1846–48

In 1846, the Oregon Territory, long in dispute with Great Britain, was finally acquired by peaceful compromise. The emigrant families who had passed Scotts Bluff had ensured this outcome by tipping the scales of population! Meanwhile, in May 1846, the United States had declared war on Mexico and, in the name of "manifest destiny," set about adding California and the Southwest to its territory.

The emigration of 1846 was lighter than that of the preceding year. One company, the Donner party, met appalling disaster in the early autumn snows of the Sierra Nevadas. Edward Bryant, a future Governor of California, and J. Quinn Thornton both wrote the most extravagant and fanciful descriptions of Scotts Bluff and nearby hills. They imagined "the ruins of some ancient vast city," complete with domes, towers, temples, minarets, amphitheaters, frowning parapets, and even "a royal bath," a fittingly picturesque backdrop for the lingering death of "the unhappy trapper" who crawled here after being abandoned by "inhuman companions."

In 1846 young historian Francis Parkman, whose journal, *The Oregon Trail,* would become one of the classics of our literature, made his famous trip to Fort Laramie. After camping "by the well-known spring on Scott's Bluff" he rode out in the morning and "descending the western side of the bluff," came upon "old Smoke's lodges." Here he launches into his first exciting description of a Sioux encampment, with its handsome lazy warriors, dusky maidens, and the "old withered crones" who did all the work!

Also in 1846, after mob violence against their city of Nauvoo, Ill., the Mormons began their great western trek. They encamped for the winter on the Missouri at Kanesville (Council Bluffs) and Winter Quarters (Omaha), where hundreds died of disease and exposure. In the spring of 1847 the mormon pioneers, 144 strong under Brigham Young, traveled to their promised land, Great Salt Lake Valley in Utah. Avoiding the "gentiles" who followed the Oregon Trail up the south bank of the Platte, the Mormons remained on the north bank until they reached Fort Laramie, using the old trappers' trail to Fort Atkinson. Probably no expedition in history has been better chronicled. Among the many meticulous Mormon journalists was William Clayton, who later wrote one of the better trail guides. On May 27 he reported that the company "passed the meridian of the northernmost peaks of Scott's Bluffs." The view toward these bluffs, "resembling ancient ruins," was "majestic and sublime."

The mormon emigration almost monopolized the trail in 1848. Some 4,000 of the faithful journeyed to Utah up the north bank, opposite the bluff, while a comparative handful of emigrants followed the usual route to Oregon. But this was the quiet before the storm. In 1848 James Marshall discovered gold on Captain Sutter's ranch. The news traveled by fast clipper ship around Cape Horn to New York City. The California gold rush would soon burst in a torrent up the North Platte migration corridor.

Scotts Bluff and the Forty-niners

Early in the spring the Forty-niners converged by steamboat upon the Missouri River towns of Independence, Westport, and St. Joseph; assembled wagons, animals, and provisions; and organized into companies. Eager to reach the new Eldorado, they were undismayed by the prospective 2,000-mile trek across hostile plains and mountains. On May 1, as soon as the prairie grass was green, the great gold rush began. The Oregon Trail became the California Road.

The trail from Independence, up the Kansas and Blue Rivers, joined the trail from St. Joseph near present Marysville, Kans., then followed up the Little Blue to its source to reach the "Coast of Nebraska," historic Platte River. Just beyond was Fort Kearny, established in 1847, now commanded by the same Captain Bonneville who first took wagons across the Continental Divide 17 years before.

Onward from Fort Kearny the white-hooded pairie schooners crawled like an army of gigantic ants along the south bank of the Platte. The Forty-niners were awed by the vast emptiness of the treeless plains, the endless horizon, the shimmering haze, and the sudden, drenching thunderstorms. Pushing beyond the forks of the Platte, they followed the margin of the South Platte to near the present town of Ogallala, Nebr. Here, at what was called Lower California Crossing, they ferried or swam the river amid scenes of shouting confusion, then headed for the North Platte.

Hundreds of extant emigrant journals vividly describe the classic trunk route of the Oregon-California Trail up the North Platte. From the plateau the trail descended rather abruptly via steep Windlass Hill down Ash Hollow (near Lewellyn) to the river. Hugging the south bank, the trail passed many curious hills and formations which afforded welcome relief from the monotonous scenery. Courthouse and Jail Rocks near present Bridgeport, Chimney Rock near Bayard, and Scotts Bluff were among the most notable of these landmarks, which so frequently aroused poetic fancies and rapturous descriptions in emigrant journals.

At Scotts Bluff in 1849 the trail made a wide detour, south of the present monument, up Gering Valley, and over Robidoux Pass, then northwest to regain the Platte near the mouth of Horse Creek.

Sixty miles beyond the bluff the Forty-niners came to historic adobe-walled Fort Laramie (Fort John of the American Fur Company), which was in the very process of being purchased by the United States Army. The Stars and Stripes were hauled up at the fort on June 26, and the army immediately began the construction of new buildings. Pausing here only briefly to rest and obtain provisions, the emigrants continued west and north via the North Platte and the Sweetwater toward the Continental Divide, guided by such landmarks as Laramie Peak, Red Butte, Independence Rock, Devil's Gate, and Split Rock. Just beyond broad, barren South Pass, flanked by the snow-covered Wind River Mountains, the Forty-niners reached the edge of the Pacific drainage. They still had a grueling journey over mountain and desert before they would reach the end of their rainbow.

Cavalcade of the Forty-Niners. Note the many forms of transportation used by travelers.

The California gold rush of 1849 and ensuing years, in addition to being on a much larger scale, was entirely different in character from the earlier Oregon migration. Oregon travelers were families, seeking farms; most of the California emigrants were young men, unmarried or unaccompanied by wives, who were seeking a quick fortune. Young women who did make the hazardous journey were besieged with suitors. There were weddings and honeymoons on the trail. There are also records of gold rush babies born in wagon beds.

After a rugged day on the trail, the evening campfire was often the occasion for yarn-swapping and sentimental songs, like *Oh, Susanna!* It can be imagined that these campfire scenes were commonplace at Scotts Bluff, and the tale of Hiram Scott's tragic death was doubtless repeated with endless variations. The prevailing mood was not always gay. The haunting mystery of Scotts Bluff struck a fittingly somber note for the Forty-niners. Before the epic drama of the gold-rush was played out a few years later, 20,000 of these adventurous emigrants had died and lined the California Road with their graves.

Asiatic cholera was the greatest killer. Ships docking at New Orleans brought infected people who carried the dread disease by steamboat up the Mississippi to St. Louis. There, the disease spread by contagion to people in the Missouri River outfitting towns. As the tired Argonauts struggled across the unfamiliar Nebraska landscape, the disease raced like wildfire among them, decimating their number.

Children were orphaned. The husband who buried his wife might himself be dead the next day. Numerous diaries record inscriptions on the crude headboards of the hastily dug shallow graves. Hundreds of burials took place in the North Platte Valley between Ash Hollow and Fort Laramie. Several have been identified at Scotts Bluff.

Many of those who escaped the cholera plague were confronted with other killers—the rugged terrain, inexperience, carelessness, exhaustion. Some dropped by the wayside from sheer fatigue. Others died of penumonia, or were drowned at the river crossings, or shot themselves with unfamiliar firearms, got run over by the big lumbering wagon wheels, or were gored by unruly oxen. Another menace was the buffalo, which was hunted as a fine source of food. Unless approached gingerly, big herds of these creatures would sometimes stampede, making the earth tremble, trampling to death the unwary hunter. In the desert of the Great Basin, more of the travelers were killed by the intense heat, alkali dust, and parching thirst. The trek of the Forty-niners was not for long a gay escapade; it became a grim survival of the fittest.

Contrary to popular impression, the number of emigrants who died at the hands of marauding Indians was negligible. The Diggers along the Humboldt River in Nevada accounted for some stragglers; the Plains Indians were a bit thievish but peaceful—for a time, at least.

True, at nights the wagons were arranged in a circular compound and guards were posted; but an Indian attack on the emigrants Hollywood style, was a rarity.

Although visions of an Indian raid served as a healthy influence on emigrant vigilance, daily preoccupation with the necessities of life was a more pressing concern. There were three primary needs—food, grazing, and good campsites. Although some of the better organized companies had ample provisions, many others miscalculated and suffered accordingly. True, buffalo, antelope, and other game were hunted; but the widlife was frightened by the endless, noisy, dusty column, and the hunters who galloped forth with romantic notions of a dashing buffalo hunt often came back empty-handed.

The ideal campsite would boast a good spring and a generous supply of timber for campfires and the repair of wagon gear. There were a few such campsites—Scotts Bluff with its springs and its ponderosa pine and cedars was one of the best—but these soon suffered from the pressure of converging crowds. Clear springs were muddied, the sparse groves of timber were chopped away, and the grass vanished from overgrazing or withered in the summer sun.

The emigrant guidebooks—Hastings, Fremont, Joseph Ware, and others—were usually adequate as a rough index to the whereabouts of obvious landmarks and choice campsites, but they were deficient in sound advice to the tenderfoot. It wasn't always possible to reach

Music at Chimney Rock was a break from the monotonous trail life.

a good campsite, and then one had to camp out on the prairie, conserving the precious water supply and eating a cold supper. Smart emigrants learned the old trappers' practice of gathering *bois du vache* (dried buffalo dung) to make an acrid but usable campfire.

A typical wagon train with all its encumbrances, plus quicksand, mud, creek crossings, and other difficulties of terrain, could make but 15 to 20 miles per day over the level plains. In rough mountain country, progress was even slower; and there had to be frequent halts to rest worn-out, emaciated stock and to mend faulty gear. Thus it took perhaps 4 months for a train to reach a California gold camp. (Starting on May 15, the crest of the migration wave would pass Scotts Bluff about mid June.) Some were later still, and had to be rescued from early snows of the Sierras. A disconsolate few would spend the winter at Fort Laramie or Salt Lake City.

Wherever and whenever they arrived, the Forty-niners were in scarecrow condition with few worldly possessions. Stoves, anvils, plows, furniture, and hardware of every description were thrown overboard from prairie schooners to ease the strain on the animals. Often this sacrifice was in vain; dead horses and oxen, littered the road to California gold.

How many Forty-niners? The population of California increased some 40,000 in 1849; it is estimated that 15,000 sailed around Cape Horn or made sailing connections at Panama; of 30,000 who went overland, perhaps 5,000 died en route. In seven succeeding years, 1850–56, the California gold rush was resumed each spring. No official census was possible, but a register kept at Fort Laramie helps to estimate that during the period 150,000 people journeyed overland westward. The peak year was 1852, when an estimated 50,000 emigrants poured through Scotts Bluff Pass.

Oregon-California Trail Geography at Scotts Bluff

Today the hills of the North Platte Valley are not accounted among the scenic wonders of the United States; in Oregon Trail days, to emigrants who had been bored with the flatness and drabness of the Platte scenery, and who would be too exhausted later to appreciate the grandeur of the Rocky Mountains, the landmarks along the Platte had a captivating charm. Courthouse Rock and Chimney Rock were the appetizers; Scotts Bluff was the grand climax.

A typical journal entry of 1849 is that of Alonzo Delano:

> June 9: The wind blew cold and unpleasant as we left our pretty encampment this morning for Scott's Bluff, a few miles beyond. The bare hills and water-worn rocks on our left began to assume many fantastic shapes, and after raising a gentle elevation, a most extraordinary sight presented

itself to our view. A basin-shaped valley, bounded by high rocky hills, lay before us, perhaps twelve miles in length, by six or eight broad. The perpendicular sides of the mountains presented the appearance of castles, forts, towers, verandas, and chimneys, with a blending of Asiatic and European architecture, and it required an effort to believe that we were not in the vicinity of some ancient and deserted town. It seemed as if the wand of a magician had passed over a city, and like that in the Arabian Nights, had converted all living things to stone.

Recent research has cleared up long-standing confusion about the geography of the Oregon-California Trail in the vicinity of Scotts Bluff. Today Scotts Bluff is understood to mean the large bluff within the national monument, between the river badlands and Mitchell Pass, which separates it from a ridge extending westward at a right angle; about 10 miles south of the river, parallel to this ridge, lies the Wildcat Hills, which extend for over 25 miles, from Chimney Rock to Robidoux Pass (see map). Because of this modern nomenclature, some historians have misunderstood the emigrant diaries, failing to realize that in Oregon Trail days Scotts Bluff, frequently spelled "Scott's Bluffs," commonly referred to all these hills, including the Wildcat Hills. William Kelly, above-mentioned, showed remarkable acumen in likening the outline of Scotts Bluff to a shepherd's crook, with the present Wildcat Hills as the straight staff and present Scotts Bluff as the flair at the end of the crook.

Similarly, the identity of the pass at Scotts Bluff has frequently been misunderstood. In historic times there were actually two different passes here. The first, which would be at the bow of the shepherd's crook, is now called Robidoux Pass, and this was predominantly used during the period up to and including 1849. In October 1850, Government explorer Capt. Howard Stansbury, returning from Salt Lake, reported the first evidence of wagon wheels through the gap now called Mitchell Pass.

Explanation for the splitting of the Oregon-California Trail at Scotts Bluff lies in its peculiar topography. The main bluff lays like a giant whale across the valley floor, blocking the way, with impenetrable badlands between it and the river. Although the existence of Mitchell Pass was, of course, known prior to 1850, it was little used because of its rugged badlands character. Travel via Robidoux Pass involved a wide swing away from the river, beginning at a point west of present Melbeta and proceeding down present Gering Valley, south of Dome Rock. In T. H. Jefferson's *Map of the Emigrant Road,* it is called Karante Valley.

Emigrant John Brown in 1849 noted that "14 miles from Chimney Rock the road [to Robidoux Pass] leaves the river. . . . [It] lies through one of the finest valleys I ever saw and is decidedly the best twenty miles of road we have travelled." Maj. Osborne Cross, leading a company of mounted riflemen to Fort Laramie, described the ascent to

"Camp at Scott's Bluff." From *The Old Journey.* Contemporary sketch by Alfred Lambourne.

Mitchell Pass looking west. Courtesy, Downey's Midwest Studio, Scottsbluff, Nebr.

Robidoux Pass as *"the first high hill* since leaving Fort Leavenworth. This is partly covered with cedar, which was the first we had met on the march."

It is suspected that the U. S. Army Quartermaster from Fort Laramie was the first to take wagons through Mitchell Pass, possibly doing a little engineering to widen the passage and ease the grade. Later emigrants, finding wagon tracks now going toward Mitchell Pass, readily switched to the new route. The two branches came together once more east of Horse Creek.

During the summer migration of 1850, equal in volume to that of 1849, the Robidoux Pass route up Gering Valley was still favored. Bennett Clark refers to his "encampment within a semicircle of high bluffs, which rise abruptly from the river's edge and sweep around rain-bow like." To Franklin Street this camp at Scotts Bluff was "one of the most delightful places that nature ever formed." To Thomas Woodward, "Every place seems like a fairy vision. It is no use trying to describe [Scotts Bluff] for language cannot do it." To Mormon emigrant Leander V. Loomis the view of the bluffs from the north side of the river was "highly beautiful, almost approaching the sublime." His journal contains this delectable entry of May 30:

> This morning there arose a heavy clowd between us and Scotts Bluff, which hid it entirely from view, and as it rolled away Showing first its lofty peak, which ascended Some 300 feet in the air, and which was covered with Small Pine or cedar trees, the scene was highly Novel, and no less beautiful we could see as it were, standing upon a clowd, a huge rock, covered with small trees, and as the clowd would rise and fall, it presented mutch the appearance of a Theater, the trees presented the appearance of the actors, the Rock, of the Stage—the clowd of the curtain, and nature itself was the tragedy they were Acting, each one playing there parts to perfection.

In 1851 use between the two passes was perhaps equally divided. William C. Lobenstine writes:

> . . . We approached the Scotch Bluffs [sic], which we saw the evening before golden in the light of the setting sun, and our whole attention was attracted by the grandeur of the former, still more beautiful country. The appearance of these sand hills, although from far off like solid rock, has a very accurate resemblance to a fortification or stronghold of the feudal barons of the middle age, of which many a reminder is yet to be met with along the bank of the Rhine. The rock itself is separated nearly at its middle, having a pass here about fifty to sixty feet wide, ascending at both sides perpendicular to a height of three to four hundred feet. The passage through here was only made possible in 1851 and is now preferred by nearly all the emigrants, cutting off a piece of eight miles from the old road. We passed through without any difficulty and after having passed another blacksmith shop and trading post, which are very numerous, protection being secured to them by the military down at Fort Laramie, we encamped for the night.

"Scott's Bluffs." From Richard Burton's *City of the Saints,* 1860.

With the migration of 1852, the historical spotlight permanently shifted to Mitchell Pass. During the early fifties the California migration reached its peak; the charms of Scotts Bluff and the peculiarities of the new pass were not lost on the new crop of journalists.

It was in 1852, apparently, that the little-used name "Capitol Hills" was first applied to Scotts Bluff by Hosea Horn and other guidebook writers. The origin of this name is suggested in the Sexton diary of June 10:

> Made our noon halt opposite Scott's Bluff, altogether the most symmetrical in form and the most stupendous in size of any we have seen. One of them is close in its resemblance to the dome of the Capitol in Washington.
>
> There is a pass through that is guarded on one side by Sugar Loaf Rock, on the other by one that resembles a square house with an observatory. It is certainly the most magnificent thing I ever saw.

In the *National Wagon Road,* a guidebook by W. Wadsworth based on a trip of 1852, Scotts Bluff is one of the three major landmarks described on the whole California Road: "Here is some of the most beautiful and picturesque scenery upon the whole route." Wadsworth labels the Scotts Bluff of today as "Convent Rock." In 1853 Frederick Piercy made a remarkable sketch of the bluffs, with buffalo-hunters in the foreground. He referred to these bluffs as "certainly the most remarkable sight I have seen since I left England."

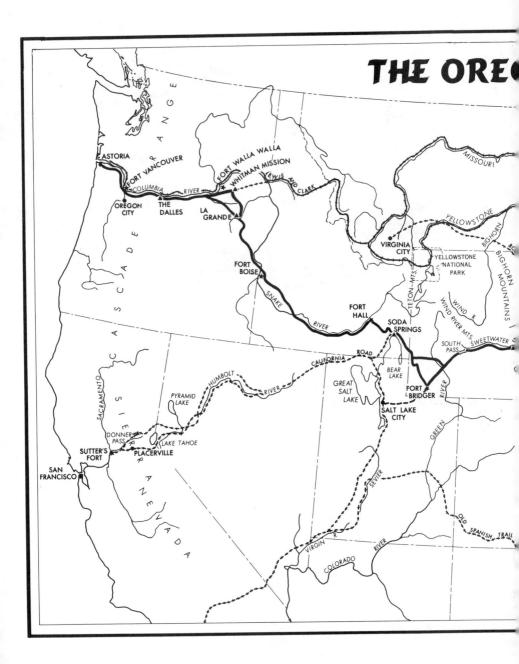

THE OREG

ON TRAIL

N

RIVER

LEWIS AND CLARK

WDER RIVER

GRAND R

BLACK HILLS

WHITE R

MISSOURI RIVER

NIOBRARA

ENCE OCK

FORT LARAMIE

LARAMIE R.

SCOTTS BLUFF

OGALLALA

JULESBURG

LOWER CALIFORNIA CROSSING

S. PLATTE

PLATTE

FORT KEARNEY

GRAND ISLAND

OMAHA

COUNCIL BLUFFS

MORMON TRAIL

NAUVOO

MISSISSIPPI

LITTLE BLUE

BIG BLUE

MARYSVILLE

ST. JOSEPH

KANSAS CITY

REPUBLICAN RIVER

KANSAS R.

INDEPENDENCE

ST. LOUIS

RIVER

COUNCIL GROVE

BENT'S FORT

SANTA FE TRAIL

PURGATOIRE

CUT-OFF

CIMARRON

N. CANADIAN

CIMARRON

ARKANSAS

S. CANADIAN

RIVER

NTA FE

APRIL 1958 NM-SB-7007

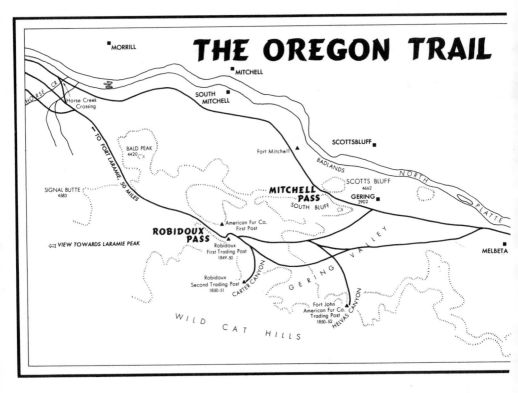

THE OREGON TRAIL

The Celinda Himes diary of 1853, describing abandoned log structures, indicates the occasional use of Robidoux Pass in later years. The Helen Carpenter journal of 1856, freely quoted in Paden *Wake of the Prairie Schooner,* clearly describes the fork in the road east of Scotts Bluff, but indicates that most people now took "the river road" through Mitchell Pass. She vividly describes also the sheer walls of Mitchell Pass, the excellent view to be had from the "summit" of the pass, the many inscriptions in the clay (long since vanished), and a soldier's grave on the side of the bluff.

To summarize, Robidoux Pass, 8 miles west of monument headquarters, was used by the Forty-niners and most of those who preceded them, including the fur traders, the emigrants to Oregon, Francis Parkman, Kearny's Dragoons, and the regiment of mounted riflemen under Maj. Winslow F. Sanderson who in 1849 rode to take over Fort Laramie. Robidoux Pass has historical primacy as "the first Scott's Bluffs Pass." On the other hand, "the second Scott's Bluffs Pass," now known as Mitchell Pass, was used by 150,000 or more emigrants, soldiers, and freighters of the 1850's and 1860's. And it was also the scene of the overland stage, the Pony Express, and the first transcontinental telegraph. Honors are about equally divided.

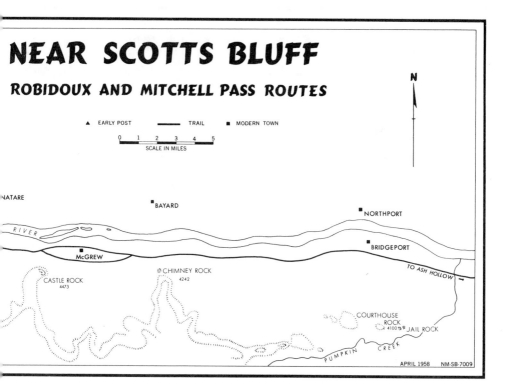

NEAR SCOTTS BLUFF

ROBIDOUX AND MITCHELL PASS ROUTES

N

▲ EARLY POST   ——— TRAIL   ■ MODERN TOWN

0 1 2 3 4 5
SCALE IN MILES

NATARE

■ BAYARD

■ NORTHPORT

RIVER

■ BRIDGEPORT

McGREW

CHIMNEY ROCK
4242

CASTLE ROCK
4473

TO ASH HOLLOW

COURTHOUSE
ROCK
4100 JAIL ROCK

PUMPKIN CREEK

APRIL 1958   NM-SB-7009

Gold Rush Trading Posts at Scotts Bluff

The big climax years for Robidoux Pass were 1849–51. A surprisingly large number of emigrant journals for these years have survived and most of them devote a lot of attention to (1) the magnificent scenery of Scotts Bluff, (2) the unusually fine springs and ample firewood here, (3) the view from the crest of the pass toward Laramie Peak (then sometimes called "the Black Hills," and frequently mistaken for the Rocky Mountains), and (4) Robidoux's log cabin blacksmith shop and trading post, and its colorful inhabitants.

Again, recent research, involving journals, Government records, and interviews with Indian descendants, has uncovered facts concerning the Robidoux establishment which have long been wrapped in obscurity. In 1849 emigrant J. Goldsborough Bruff noted "a cool clear spring and brook" in the deep gulch around which the wagons had to detour. "Close by is a group of Indian lodges and tents, surrounding a log cabin, where you can buy whisky for $5 per gallon; and look at the *beautiful* squaws, of the traders."

Another illuminating description is that given by Captain Stansbury on his westward trip of 1849:

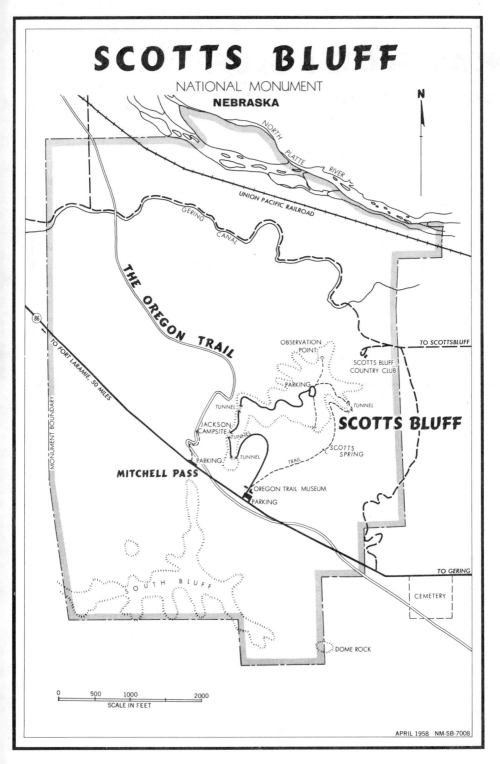

SCOTTS BLUFF
NATIONAL MONUMENT
NEBRASKA

N

NORTH PLATTE RIVER

UNION PACIFIC RAILROAD

GERING CANAL

THE OREGON TRAIL

86

TO FORT LARAMIE, 50 MILES

MONUMENT BOUNDARY

OBSERVATION POINT

TO SCOTTSBLUFF

SCOTTS BLUFF COUNTRY CLUB

PARKING

TUNNEL

TUNNEL

JACKSON CAMPSITE

TUNNEL

SCOTTS BLUFF

SCOTTS SPRING

PARKING

TUNNEL

TRAIL

MITCHELL PASS

OREGON TRAIL MUSEUM

PARKING

TO GERING

SOUTH BLUFF

CEMETERY

DOME ROCK

0   500   1000   2000
SCALE IN FEET

APRIL 1958   NM-SB-7008

34

Robidoux's second trading post at "Scott's Bluffs."   Sketch by Möllhausen, 1851.

. . . Three miles from the Chimney Rock, the road gradually leaves the river for the purpose of passing behind Scott's Bluff, a point where a spur from the main ridge comes so close to the river as to leave no room for the passage of teams.   There was no water between these two points, a distance of more than twenty miles, and we were consequently obliged to go on until nine o'clock, when we encamped at the bluff, on a small run near a delicious spring, after having been in the saddle sixteen hours without food, and travelled thirty-one and a-half miles.   The march was a severe one upon the animals, as they were in harness, after the noon halt, for seven successive hours, without water.   The afternoon was oppressively hot, and the gnats and musquitoes almost insufferable.   There is a temporary blacksmith's shop here, established for the benefit of the emigrants, but especially for that of the owner, who lives in an Indian lodge, and had erected a log shanty by the roadside, in one end of which was the blacksmith's forge, and in the other a grog-shop and sort of grocery.   The stock of this establishment consisted principally of such articles as the owner had purchased from the emigrants at a great sacrifice and sold to others at as great a profit.   Among other things, an excellent double wagon was pointed out to me, which he had purchased for seventy-five cents.   The blacksmith's shop was an equally profitable concern; as, when the smith was indisposed to work himself, he rented the use of shop and tools for the modest price of seventy-five cents an

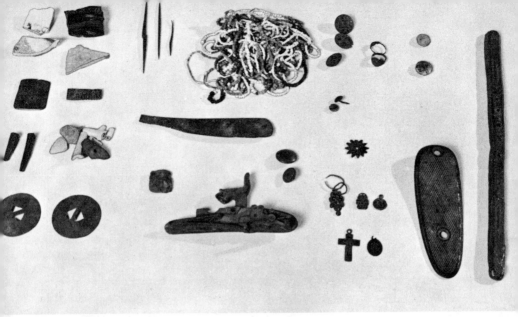

Historical objects from site of Robidoux's trading post.

hour, and it was not until after waiting for several hours that I could get the privilege of shoeing two of the horses, even at that price, the forge having been in constant use by the emigrants. Scott's Bluff, according to our measurement, is five hundred and ninety-six miles from Fort Leavenworth, two hundred and eighty-five from Fort Kearny, and fifty-one from Fort Laramie.

Others wryly note the shrewdness of this makeshift proprietor, Robidoux. Various journalists refer to two or more "Frenchmen" and their squaws, and an indefinite number of children. In 1850 James Bennett found here "an encampment of near a 100 Sioux Indians" (relatives, no doubt!). In 1851 Father De Smet, returning from the Horse Creek Treaty Council, baptized Robidoux's halfbreed children.

In 1851, Robidoux, feeling somewhat overrun by the emigrant hordes, retired to a secluded canyon about a mile southeast of the original location. The appearance of this second trading post has been providentially preserved in a sketch by the German traveler, Frederick Mollhausen. The site of this post has been identified in present Carter Canyon.

Who was Robidoux? Although all the facts are not fully established, it appears that he was Joseph E. Robidoux, oldest son of the Joseph Robidoux who founded St. Joseph, Mo.; and that the other "Frenchman" seen there was his uncle, Antoine Robidoux, who earlier achieved pioneering fame in Utah and California. The younger

Joseph is an elusive figure. He may well have been the Robidoux who led the first American Fur Company contingent by Scotts Bluff, in 1830, and who was seen at Fort Laramie in 1846 by Parkman.

What became of Robidoux? Although reported to have died accidentally at Scotts Bluff, no grave has been identified. There is evidence that he returned to the Great Nemaha Indian Agency, in northeastern Kansas, in the late fifties, and died there in obscurity. There are many half-breed "Robidouxes" on Indian reservations in South Dakota who have identified the Scotts Bluff Robidoux as their ancestor.

Modern research has revealed another fact long lost sight of. Robidoux's trading post was not the only one in this neighborhood during the gold rush. It has now been definitely established that, in the summer of 1849, after they sold adobe-walled Fort John (Fort Laramie) to the U. S. Government, officials of the American Fur Company removed to Scotts Bluff. Contrary to a long-held erroneous impression, their new post was not located near Mitchell Pass (there never was a trading post near there); it was first located tentatively in Robidoux Pass, within a few hundred yards of Robidoux's blacksmith shop. Then, for reasons which can only be surmised, it was moved to a point 6 miles below Robidoux's and 8 miles south of Mitchell Pass, in present Helvas Canyon. In correspondence of the fur company it was identified as "Fort John, Scott's Bluffs."

This post, being off the main trail, did not rate much notice by travelers, compared with the attention given to Robidoux, but there are occasional references. In 1850 James Bennett states that about 7 miles below Robidoux's there was a trading post "3 miles to our left, where we could see a herd of cattle grazing." Sgt. Percival G. Lowe of the Dragoons, in 1850, reports that "we turned south and camped near a trading post belonging to Major Dripps."

Andrew Drips, the "mountain man" who had guided De Smet up this way in 1840, was later replaced by Joseph Papin of St. Louis, who died and was buried here. His grave and the outlines of the second "Fort John" have been identified. It is not known just when this place was abandoned. However, when the main artery of traffic definitely moved from Robidoux to Mitchell Pass, in 1852, "Fort John" and Robidoux's post both doubtless "withered on the vine," in the manner of a modern-day filling station which is by-passed by a new highway.

Collections of historical objects found on the surface of the sites of Robidoux's two posts and "Fort John, Scott's Bluffs" are preserved in the Oregon Trail Museum. Beads, pendants, danglers, belts, buttons, medallions, coins, traps, bar lead, bullet molds, and other objects testify to the variety of activities conducted at these stations. Although long consigned to oblivion, these primitive commercial establishments were the true beginnings of private enterprise in the Scotts Bluff area.

Coming of the Bullwhackers

The Grattan massacre of 1854 and retaliation by Harney's forces in 1855 were prologues to the inevitable showdown with the Plains Indians discussed later. New posts were built, garrisons were strengthened, and expeditions were launched. In 1857 troops had to be sent to Utah to quell the rebellious Mormons; at the same time the Cheyennes staged an outbreak. It became necessary for the Government to move huge quantities of equipment and provisions westward up the Platte Valley, and the freighting contractors came into the picture. Notable among these was the firm of Russell, Majors, and Waddell of Kansas City (old Westport).

The army freight moved in huge Conestoga wagons drawn by 6 to 8 teams of oxen. A new profession arose known as "bullwhacker" and we can well imagine the bedlam that accompanied the passage of a "bulltrain" or the process of yoking up the bellowing animals in the morning after the nightly encampment in the wagon compound. The experience of taking a bulltrain through Mitchell Pass is vividly described by T. S. Kenderdine in 1858:

> Passing over a dreary country, which barely furnished enough of grass for our famished animals, we arrived at Scott's Bluffs on the afternoon of the 25th. This is a bold escarpment of sand and clay, about a half a mile in length and near a thousand feet in height, extending southward from the river and rising like a gigantic barrier to obstruct our way. It was for a long time visible, and at a distance seemed impossible to be surmounted. The road forks before we reach the bluffs, one trail passing around its southern end and re-joining the main road at some distance beyond it, the other passing directly over its summit. The latter is the worse road of the two, but it being the shorter, we chose it. We were detained some time at the foot of the bluff by the breaking of one of our wagons, but we at last got under way, and commenced our toilsome journey over it. The ascent was easy and gradual, until we came to a deep gorge, which intersected our road at the foot of the main bluff. Crossing this at the imminent risk of being run over by the teams as they plunged headlong to the bottom, we came to a series of steep hills and narrow, deep and sandy defiles, through which there was barely room for a wagon to pass. So squarely hewn were some of these passes, that one could hardly believe that art had not a hand in their formation. After a vast deal of exertion we at last reached the summit, when we commenced the still more dangerous descent. Tumbling pell-mell down narrow passages, slowly crawling over abrupt ascents, we at length reached the bottom, and in two miles struck the river and encamped, but not till long after dark.

In 1857, the year of the Utah War, there was quite a crop of Scotts Bluff enthusiasts. Cornelius Conway, a freighter with the Utah Expedition, went into raptures over the scenery. He refers to Mitchell Pass as "Devil's Gap," because of its tortuous passage. Capt. Jesse A. Gove tells of passing through "the celebrated Scott's Bluff, a cut of

Freighters at Independence Rock. These huge Conestogas often carried up to 4,000 pounds of supplies.

some 7 miles from the old road." Being rear guard, he had time to "sketch the notch." In 1857, according to Capt. Randolph Marcy's guidebook, *The Prairie Traveller,* from the pass "the road descends the mountain, at the foot of which is the Platte and a mail station."

William A. Carter, civilian trader bound for Fort Bridger with a U. S. Army contingent, noted the "gigantic mass" of Scotts Bluff, which split the trail. The old road to the left was taken by the troops, but Carter himself was advised

> . . . to take the straight forward road leading through the chain of Bluffs and descending by a nearer rout to the Platt again. This, we afterwards regretted as we got through the pass with great difficulty—we found a large freight [wagon] stopped in the pass, the mud being very deep. The axle of one wagon was broken and a dying ox lying crippled in the road—The bellowing of the Ox which reverberated along the bluff—and the croaking of the thousands of Ravens that were hovering over, had a gloomy and ominous sound. This pass is truly a wonder. The bluffs here form a semi circle and on each side rise up into huge towers which make the head dizzy to look up at. The passage through is level, but has been cut into deep ravines by the torrents which run down the sides of the Bluffs.

The mystic spell that Scotts Bluff seemed to weave about early travelers continued unbroken during the following decade. Perhaps the high point in romantic imagination was reached in 1860 by the English adventurer, Richard Burton:

> . . . In the dull uniformity of the prairies, it is a striking and attractive object, far excelling the castled crag of Drachenfels or any of the beauties of romantic Rhine. . . . As you approach within four or five miles, a massive medieval city gradually defines itself, clustering, with a wonderful fullness of detail, round a colossal fortress, and crowned with a royal

William H. Jackson painting of bull train in Mitchell Pass based on original sketch of 1866.

castle. . . . At a nearer aspect again, the quaint illusion vanishes. The lines of masonry become yellow layers of boulder and pebble imbedded in a mass of stiff, tamped, bald, marly clay; the curtains and angles change to the gashings of the rain of ages, and the warriors are metamorphosed into dwarf cedars and dense shrubs, scattered singly over the surface. . . .

The Sioux uprising of the 1860's kept pleasure travel to a minimum, but even U. S. soldiers, intent on hammering the redskins, gave pause to express wonder at "the Gibraltar of the Plains." For the first time we have evidence of travelers clambering up the sloping side to the summit of the bluff, to survey the countryside. In 1862 Burlingame described the view as "a scene seldom vouchsafed to mortals." The following year A. B. Ostrander, a drummer boy with the volunteer infantry, laboriously scaled the cliffs, then scrambled hastily down again to catch up with his regiment when he thought he saw Indians.

Also in 1863 Benjamin M. Connor made note of the wind wailing dismally through the gap, which he erroneously called "Marshall's Pass, for a captain of my company." Guide Jim Bridger, who had been one of the first white men to see Scotts Bluff, back in the 1820's, told Connor that the bluff "was named for a man who saved his life from pursuing Indians by taking refuge in the cliffs." Bridger, who had been an associate of Hiram Scott, must have known better.

"Yoking Up." From original sketch by William H. Jackson.

Scotts Bluff—The Artistic Record

The last noteworthy Oregon Trail journalist was a young "bull-whacker" of 1866 named William H. Jackson, who was destined to become the "living link" between Scotts Bluff National Monument and its historic past. When he came to Mitchell Pass he found the going tough. He reports that "we had one of the steepest and worst gulches to drive through that we have yet had." His outfit camped just west of the pass. Finding no spring in the vicinity, someone had to go 3 miles to the river for water. Young Jackson, a man of notable artistic talent, stopped to sketch the pass. Today, nearly a century later, his original sketch of Mitchell Pass, together with dozens of his other original Oregon Trail sketches and paintings, hang in the William H. Jackson Room of the Oregon Trail Museum.

William H. Jackson achieved fame as the "Pioneer Photographer" of the Rocky Mountain West, being the first to make a photographic record of Yellowstone geysers, the Teton Mountains, and many other scenic wonders now preserved in National Parks. In 1936, at the age of 93, he accepted an invitation to make the dedication speech for the history wing of the new museum-administration building. In 1938 on a visit here he staked out his 1866 campsite, which is now identified by a trailside marker. After his death in 1943 the American Pioneer Trails Association donated many of Jackson's original sketches and later watercolors to the National Park Service, while Julius F. Stone donated $10,000 as the nucleus of a fund to build a Jackson

Memorial Room. The building fund was supplemented by public contributions and the completed wing was dedicated in 1949.

The A. J. Miller sketch of 1837 and the Jackson sketch of 1866, the earliest and the latest known pictures of Scotts Bluff made during Oregon Trail days, are the best known today. The Piercy sketch of 1853, above noted, has been rather widely reprinted. Other authentic contemporary drawings are found only in obscure or rare out-of-print guidebooks or journals. Noteworthy among these are those of David Leeper in 1849, Benjamin Ferris in 1854, Cornelius Conway in 1857, T. S. Kenderdine in 1858, Richard Burton in 1860, and Alfred Lambourne, date uncertain.

Pony Express to Iron Horse, 1860–69

The California gold rush had not yet abated when strikes of precious metals were made in Nevada and Colorado (1858-59), later in Montana and Idaho (1864). The result was a ramification of the old Oregon-California Trail, with major branches up the South Platte to Denver, and from Fort Laramie northward along the Bighorn Mountains to Virginia City, Mont. (the Bozeman Trail). The new mining communities added their demands to those of Utah and California for improved communication with the States. In the fifties and sixties Scotts Bluff witnessed dramatic changes.

The first mail service up the Platte route was inaugurated by the Mormons; after the army occupied Fort Laramie, military dispatches were carried on regular schedules to Eastern command posts. Public mail service to California began in 1851. By 1860 the Central Overland and Pike's Peak Express Company held a monopoly on mail contracts between the Missouri and the Pacific.

No frontier institution better dramatizes the spirit of American enterprise than the famed Pony Express, fast biweekly mail service. From April 1860 to October 1861 youthful riders on fleet mustangs pounded between St. Joseph, Mo., and Hangtown (Placerville), Calif., braving the elements and Indian dangers. William Russell of the freighting firm was the promoter of the Pony Express. Although financially disastrous, it demonstrated the need for Government mail subsidies.

Pony Express stations were about 15 miles apart and each rider made up to 100 miles at a time, changing to fresh ponies at each station. Stations in the Scotts Bluff vicinity were at Chimney Rock, near present Melbeta (the Scotts Bluff Station at Ficklin Spring, named for a company official), and at Horse Creek. The Scotts Bluff Station, made of massive adobe walls, later became the Mark Coad Ranch. The thrill of watching a Pony Express rider gallop past is

View southeast from summit of Scotts Bluff to Dome Rock. Gering Valley (Robidoux Pass Route) in background.

Scotts Bluff from the Mormon Trail. Courtesy, Downey's Midwest Studio, Scottsbluff, Nebr.

Changing mounts at Pony Express Station. Original sketch in Oregon Trail Museum.

vividly described in *Roughing It* by Mark Twain, who was a statecoach passenger bound for Nevada. The incident took place just east of the pass at Scotts Bluff.

> We had had a consuming desire, from the beginning, to see a pony-rider, but somehow or other all that passed us and all that met us managed to streak by in the night, and so we heard only a whiz and a hail, and the swift phantom of the desert was gone before we could get our heads out of the windows. But now we were expecting one along every moment, and would see him in broad daylight. Presently the driver exclaims:
>
> "HERE HE COMES!"
>
> Every neck is stretched further, and every eye strained wider. Away across the endless dead level of the prairie a black speck appears against the sky, and it is plain that it moves. Well, I should think so! In a second or two it becomes a horse and rider, rising and falling, rising and falling—sweeping toward us nearer and nearer—growing more and more distinct, more and more sharply defined—nearer and still nearer, and the flutter of the hoofs comes faintly to the ear—another instant a whoop and a hurrah from our upper deck, a wave of the rider's hand, but no reply, and man and horse burst past our excited faces, and go swinging away like a belated fragment of a storm!

The first transcontinental telegraph line, up the Platte route through Mitchell Pass, ended the meteoric Pony Express. In 1860 Edward Creighton of the Pacific Telegraph Company had reconnoitered the Oregon Trail via Mitchell Pass. The active construction of the line took but a few months, in 1861, and in October telegrams were going to California. Service in the early days was hampered by

Indians, suspicious of the "singing wires," who frequently burned down the poles. There was an early telegraph station at Fort Mitchell, at the foot of Scotts Bluff.

In 1861, Russell, Majors, and Waddell subcontracted with the Butterfield Overland Mail Company to operate overland stage and mail service over the Central Route (moved up from the Southwest because of the imminent Civil War). There was daily coach service to California via Scotts Bluff until 1862, when Indian troubles required the new operator, Benjamin Holladay, to transfer the route southward, via Lodgepole Creek and Elk Mountain. The days of the famed Concord stage in the Scotts Bluff area were short lived.

As the telegraph made the Pony Express obsolete, so the railroad spelled the doom of the stagecoach and the prairie schooner. The easy gradient over the Continental Divide at South Pass was the geographic reason for the centrally located Oregon Trail. However, political rather than geographic reasons dictated the central location of the first transcontinental railroad. During the 1850's there were many "Pacific Railroad Surveys" which did much to fill in the blank pages of Western topography, but none of these touched the North Platte. At the outbreak of the Civil War, President Lincoln decided that a central overland railroad would strengthen the ties of the

The advancing telegraph ended the short-lived Pony Express in June of 1861.

Union. It was in August 1865, however, before the seasoned engineer and Indian fighter, Gen. Grenville M. Dodge, made his reconnaissance for the future Union Pacific Railroad. Although the route finally selected followed Lodgepole Creek to Cheyenne Pass, the general did examine the North Platte, pausing to sketch Mitchell Pass on August 27. The "iron horse" reached Cheyenne in 1867, and joined the Central Pacific with due ceremony at Promontory Point, Utah, May 10, 1869. This date can be accepted as marking the end of the historic Oregon-California Trail.

Warfare on the Plains

In the early 1860's the mounted eagle-plumed warriors of the plains, including the Sioux and Cheyenne, went on the warpath. Scotts Bluff looked down upon many exciting scenes of conflict.

During the days of the trapper and the emigrant, the Indian had been generally peaceful, despite occasional pilferings and "greenhorn" alarms. Indeed, many white traders, such as Robidoux, had freely intermarried with the Indians. The migration of 1849, giving evidence of the white man's strength, coupled with his wanton slaughter of the life-giving buffalo, caused some uneasiness among the tribes. In October 1850, Col. E. V. Sumner with a company of mounted infantry en route to Fort Laramie met and counseled with one band of Sioux at Scotts Bluff. They, like their red brethren throughout the plains, were full of complaints. To quiet them, old mountain man Thomas Fitzpatrick, Indian agent for the Upper Platte, engineered the greatest Indian peace council ever held on the Plains. This was at Horse Creek, a few miles west of Scotts Bluff.

In September 1851 around 10,000 Indians from the tribes of the Sioux, Cheyenne, Arapaho, Crow, Snake, Ree, Gros Ventre, and Assiniboin assembled at Fort Laramie. The U. S. Government was represented by Fitzpatrick; the famed missionary, Father De Smet; Robert Campbell (one of the founders of Fort Laramie); and D. D. Mitchell, superintendent of Indian Affairs at St. Louis. Jim Bridger and other oldtimers showed up to help keep peace among traditional enemies. Because there was not grass enough for the horses of this vast assemblage, the council moved downriver. It was an historic occasion with much colorful pageantry. The negotiations went smoothly, and by "the First Treaty of Fort Laramie" the Indians promised to permit peaceful passage of travelers through their domain in exchange for an annuity of $50,000 in provisions and trade goods.

This peace treaty, like so many others, was soon broken. In August 1854 a misunderstanding between an Oglala Sioux and a Mormon emigrant, compounded by the inexperience of Lt. John L. Grat-

"The Gorge, Scott's Bluff." From Perkins' *Trails, Rails and War.* Sketch by Dodge, 1865.

tan from Fort Laramie, led to the massacre of Grattan, 30 soldiers, and his interpreter 8 miles east of Fort Laramie.   This was "avenged" in September 1855 by the slaughter of innocent Brule Indians by an expeditionary force under Gen. William S. Harney, near Ash Hollow. En route to Fort Laramie, the cavalrymen trooped through Mitchell Pass with over 200 fresh Indian scalps in their baggage.

In 1862 there was a bloody uprising of the Minnesota Sioux.   Hostilities spread to the Plains, with grave danger to lines of communication and army outposts with garrisons depleted by the Civil War. During this period, Fort Laramie was a headquarters post, occupied during the crucial years principally by the 11th Ohio Volunteer Cavalry, under Col. William O. Collins.   There was a chain of outposts up and down the North Platte, from Mud Springs near present Bridgeport to South Pass, Wyo.   These were frequently harassed by

Sioux and Cheyenne warriors. One of these beleaguered outposts was adobe-walled Fort Mitchell, about 2 miles northwest of Mitchell Pass.

Initially called "Camp Shuman" for its builder and first commander, Capt. J. S. Shuman, it was constructed in 1864, according to official records, and was last heard of in 1867. The little fort (and later nearby "Scott's Bluffs Pass") was named for Brig. Gen. Robert B. Mitchell (1823–82), commander of the Nebraska Military District, a citizen of Kansas Territory who earlier fought gallantly in the Civil War and later became Governor of New Mexico Territory. Fort Mitchell saw its share of frontier action. Colonel Collins' report of 1865 to the regimental adjutant advises:

> Co H has been Stationed at Fort Mitchell 55 Miles East of Laramie on the Platte River. The company participated in the celebrated Indian fights at Mud Springs and Rush Creek where 150 Men under Command of Lt Col Wm O Collins fought from fifteen hundred to two thousand of the dusky warriors, since that time this Company has carried the Mail from Julesberg to Laramie. This has been heavy and laborious duty, yet they have never flinched but have had the Mail through in good time. Besides this company has built one Mail Station, near the noted Land Mark Chimney Rock, besides repairing the one at Mud Springs.

Cavalrymen leaving Fort Mitchell. The small, adobe-walled outpost was active from August 1864 to November 1867.

William H. Jackson sketch of Fort Mitchell at Scotts Bluff.

The Battle of Mud Springs in February 1865 was an aftermath of the siege of Julesburg by a horde of Sioux and Cheyenne who were enraged by a massacre of Cheyennes at Sand Creek, Colo. In zero weather the small garrison at Fort Mitchell joined Colonel Collins' forces in an attempt to intercept the north-bound Indians. After skirmishing and light casualties, the Indians withdrew across the North Platte.

A second engagement near Scotts Bluff was known as the Battle of Horse Creek. In June 1865, Capt. William D. Fouts led a company of the 7th Iowa Cavalry who were escorting 185 lodges of supposedly peaceful Brule Sioux from Fort Laramie to Fort Kearny. Between Horse Creek and Fort Mitchell the Indians treacherously attacked, killing Captain Fouts and three soldiers. The Fort Mitchell garrison rode out to aid the Iowans, but again the Sioux retreated across the Platte. Colonel Moonlight at Fort Laramie, advised by telegram from Camp Mitchell, futilely pursued the Indians with a cavalry force.

Other skirmishes, including besieged wagon corrals, ambushes in Mitchell Pass, and troops from Fort Mitchell galloping to the rescue, are reported in the literature, though with scanty evidence.

Fort Mitchell was occupied at various times by units of the 11th Ohio Volunteer Cavalry, the 12th Missouri Volunteers, and the 18th U. S. Infantry. The last identifiable commander was Capt. Robert P. Hughes, of the latter regiment. He was detached there in 1866 by Col. Henry B. Carrington who, with 2,000 troops and 226 mule teams, was en route to construct posts along the Bozeman Trail in the Powder

River country. Among the few brief eyewitness descriptions which survive is this impression of Colonel Carrington's wife:

> . . . [Scott's Bluffs are] of mixed clay and sand, plentifully supplied with fossils, and throw a spur across the Platte basin so as to compel the traveler to leave the river and make a long detour to the south, or to pass through the bluffs themselves. This passage is by a tortuous gorge where wagons can seldom pass each other; and at times the drifting snows or sands almost obscure the high walls and battlements that rise several hundred feet on either side. . . .
> Almost immediately after leaving the Bluffs, and at the foot of the descent, after the gorge is passed, we find Fort Mitchell. This is a subpost of Laramie of peculiar style and compactness. The walls of the quarters are also the outlines of the fort itself, and the four sides of the rectangle are respectively the quarters of officers, soldiers, and horses, and the warehouse of supplies. Windows open into the little court or parade-ground; and bedrooms as well as all other apartments, are loopholed for defense.

All trace of Fort Mitchell has disappeared but a ground plan of the enclosure is preserved in the Collins Collection of the Colorado Agricultural College. Three authentic contemporary sketches of Fort Mitchell have been discovered; one of 1865 by an unidentified soldier of the 11th Ohio reproduced in *The Bozeman Trail;* one by an unidentified artist with the Hayden Territorial Survey of 1867, published in *U. S. Geological Survey of Wyoming,* in 1871; and the one by William H. Jackson, preserved in the Oregon Trail Museum.

Hostilities on the Plains came to a climax when Colonel Carrington built Fort Reno, Fort Phil Kearny, and Fort C. F. Smith on the Bozeman Trail. This trail extended from Fort Laramie northwestward to Virginia City, Mont., scene of a new gold rush. Capt. William J. Fetterman and 80 men were slain in an ambush in December 1866 at Fort Phil Kearny (near present Buffalo, Wyo.). In 1867 Red Cloud's warriors were repulsed at the Wagon Box and Hayfield Fights; but the Government decreed that this trail to the Montana mines must be abandoned. By the second treaty of Fort Laramie, in 1868, the Sioux were granted an extensive hunting domain between the North Platte and Missouri Rivers.

The treaty of 1868 marked the end of major Indian hostilities in the North Platte Valley. In 1870 Red Cloud was induced to visit the Great White Father (President Grant) in Washington; he was also taken to New York City, where he gave an impressive oration in his native tongue to the assembled palefaces. Red Cloud wanted an agency and trading post set up near Fort Laramie, long the traditional camp of the Oglala Sioux. The Government wanted to set up the agency far north of the Platte, on the White River. To humor the Indians, still in a resentful mood, the first Red Cloud Agency was established on the north bank of the Platte, half way between Fort Laramie and Scotts Bluff, at present Henry, Nebr., on the Wyoming

Chief Red Cloud
was a leader of
the Oglala Sioux during
the 1860s and 1870s.

boundary. This became the temporary home of more than 6,000 Dakota Sioux (mainly Oglala and Brule), 1,500 Cheyenne, and 1,300 Arapaho.

Under the prevailing peace policy the Episcopal Church took over the Sioux Agency. Their first agent was J. W. Wham. Unable to control Red Cloud and his excitable warriors, Wham was soon replaced by another churchman, J. W. Daniels. It was not easy for the victors of the Bozeman Trail war to mend their ways. The Sioux ambushed Pawnee buffalo-hunters in 1873 at Massacre Canyon on the Republican River; others joined hostiles on the Powder River in an attack on the Crow Indians and on the Northern Pacific survey parties on the Lower Yellowstone River. In 1873, Daniels finally managed to persuade these "peaceful" Indians to move the agency to White River, where Fort Robinson was established the next year.

The discovery of gold in the Black Hills in 1874, the attempt to reduce further the Sioux reservation, the swift events which culminated in the disastrous Battle of the Little Bighorn in 1876, and the subsequent rounding up of the scattered Sioux to be placed on Dakota reservations, the killing of CrazyHorse at Fort Robinson—all these events occurred far to the north of Scotts Bluff. The only "wild Indians" to appear again in this area were Dull Knife's Cheyennes, who passed here in 1878 in a spectacular northward flight from their hated reservation in Oklahoma.

Hunters, Miners, Cowboys, and Homesteaders

The ruthless hide-hunters were effective allies of the U. S. Army in ending resistance of the Plains Indian to the white man's advance. The American bison, or buffalo, had been the staff of life and the major source of food, clothing, and shelter for the Indians. Once vast buffalo herds, blackening the landscape, crossed and recrossed the North Platte River. The many expeditions and the emigrants on the California Road killed the huge shaggy beast wholesale. As a result, most of the herds withdrew to the southern Plains.

Construction of transcontinental railroads and the addition of new military posts along their route created a huge demand for fresh meat; in the East there was a good market for buffalo robes. The result was an intensive campaign of slaughter by professional hunters, armed with heavy Sharps and Ballard buffalo rifles. The stupid creatures were easy game for the hunter, who ran after them Indian fashion or calmly mowed them down from a prone position, as they grazed. In the mid-seventies the Kansas Pacific Railroad alone hauled out the carcasses of 3 million buffalo. It is estimated that more than 30 million buffalo were destroyed during the two decades, 1860–80. Descendants of the few creatures that survived this slaughter are now to be found only in zoos and in Government preserves, such as Yellowstone National Park.

The Black Hills Gold Rush of 1876 by-passed Scotts Bluff. Hopeful prospectors rode the Union Pacific Railroad to Sidney or Cheyenne, then followed trails northward to the diggings. The Sidney-Black Hills route crossed the North Platte over a private toll bridge at Camp Clarke, near modern Bridgeport. The Cheyenne-Deadwood Trail crossed a new Army-built iron truss bridge over the North Platte at Fort Laramie.

The last chapter in the pre-settlement history of Scotts Bluff could be entitled "The Cowboy Era." The open range cattle industry really began during Oregon Trail days, when sharp traders in the Fort Laramie area discovered that there was profit in exchanging one head of fat cattle for two that were worn out. They also discovered that oxen wintered well in the Laramie River Valley. Demand for cattle increased with the big Utah overland freighting business of the 1850's.

Hunting buffalo at Scotts Bluff.

Loading buffalo bones at Scotts Bluff.

Cowboys driving longhorn cattle past Scotts Bluff.

After the Civil War herds of half-wild longhorn Texas cattle were rounded up for the long drive northward to shipping points on the Kansas Pacific and Union Pacific Railways. In 1868 Texas cattle reached Kearney, North Platte, and Ogallala.

In the 1870's ranchers began to appropriate lush grazing lands in the North Platte Valley and its tributaries. It is said that by 1872 there were 60,000 head on Horse Creek, near Scotts Bluff. After the mop-up of hostile Sioux bands in 1876–77, thousands more were driven from Ogallala past Scotts Bluff toward the vast ranges in the northern Plains. Pratt and Ferris, Swan Land and Cattle Company, and the Coad Brothers were among the big outfits who grazed cattle in the Scotts Bluff area. Rapid inflation of the cattle market, overstocking and overgrazing, coupled with the disastrous hard winter of 1885–86, hastened the end of this short-lived but much publicized era.

In 1885 the first homesteaders, or grangers, arrived to stake out their claims in the Nebraska Panhandle. Gering was platted in 1888. In 1900 the Burlington Railroad was built up the north side of the Platte and the town of Scottsbluff was born. In 1910 a Union Pacific branch line was built up the south bank.

Where buffalo once roamed there are now irrigation ditches, sugar beet, alfalfa, and potato fields, and prime Herefords. The wily Sioux have become peaceful citizens. The dusty roads of the covered wagons have been replaced by broad paved highways and fast automobiles. Bullboats and Conestoga wagons have been replaced by long freight trains and cometlike aircraft. Scotts Bluff, named for one of General Ashley's fur traders, the brooding sentinel of the Oregon Trail, now belongs to history.

Natural History of Scotts Bluff

Although Scotts Bluff is primarily significant because of its historical associations, its geology and biology are also interesting. Indeed, appreciation of the history of the bluff is enhanced by an understanding of how this bluff was formed and how it influenced migration routes. An elementary knowledge of the plant and animal life of the area, which is today much as it was in the covered wagon era, adds to your understanding of this story.

Elevations. The highest point in the monument area is South Bluff, 4,692 feet above sea level. (The highest point in Nebraska, more than 5,000 feet, is in Banner County, south of Scotts Bluff.) The "high point" on Scotts Bluff proper is 4,649 feet, which is 766 feet above the North Platte River or 700 feet above the badlands at its immediate base. The elevation of monument headquarters is 4,114 feet.

Badlands at the foot of Scotts Bluff's north face. Courtesy, Union Pacific Railroad.

Geology. This bluff, like the neighboring Wildcat Hills, Chimney Rock, and Courthouse Rock, is an erosional remnant of the ancient Great Plains. These plains were formed by the deposit of gravel, sand, and silt brought down by rivers from the Rocky Mountains after they were uplifted about 60 million years ago. At intervals, 30 to 40 million years ago, volcanoes to the west also added great quantities of ash and dust deposits. When the process of deposit slowed, erosion gained headway, cutting new river valleys in the Plains. High tablelands were left on both sides of the North Platte Valley. Landmarks such as Scotts Bluff and Chimney Rock have hard rock caps that protect them from erosion.

The lower two-thirds of the bluff consists of Brule clay, an Oligocene deposit of buff-colored, soft-textured sandy clay. The badlands formation at the foot of the bluff dramatically demonstrates the rapid erosion of the Brule clay when unprotected by cap rock. The upper one-third of the bluff consists of the Arickaree formation, gray sand beds of the Miocene Epoch. The uppermost Arickaree beds form the top surface of the bluff. These are laced with hard tubular concretions which help protect the bluff and add to the resistance of the beds to weathering. All the formations exposed in the walls of the bluff are interspersed with thin layers of pinkish volcanic ash.

Paleontology. The Badlands regions of western Nebraska and South Dakota have become world famous for their extensive deposits of fossils of mammals and other animals that lived during the Oligocene and Miocene Epochs of the Cenozoic Era. The Brule clay formation of Scotts Bluff and vicinity is particularly rich in fossil remains of extinct animals of Oligocene age, 30 to 40 million years ago. These exposed remains gave rise to many Indian legends and were frequently noted by curious emigrants. Scientists from many institutions of learning have continued to explore and examine these fossils since 1847, when Dr. Hiram Prout of St. Louis described a jawbone brought to him by a fur trader as that of a *Titanothere,* a giant rhinoceros-like creature.

Among the most common fossils of the Scotts Bluff vicinity are giant turtles, pig-like *Oreodonts,* ancient forms of rhinoceroses, saber-toothed tigers, dogs, deer, camels, and rodents. The horse family is represented here by *Mesohippus,* a three-toed creature about 18 inches in height.

Plantlife. The conspicuous trees on the summit and north slopes of Scotts Bluff are ponderosa pine and a juniper usually called Rocky Mountain red cedar. In ravines and along the river banks are cottonwood, willow, and boxelder. The most common shrubs in the area are mountain-mahogany, wild currant, and wild rose. Wildflowers include sunflower, daisies, wild sweetpea, golden banner, penstemon, Indian paintbrush, yucca or soapweed, ball cactus, and prickly pear cactus. The dominant grasses are blue grama, side-oats grama, buffalo-grass, slender and western wheatgrasses, and woolly sedge.

Wildlife. During historic times the North Platte Valley was in the heart of buffalo country, but extermination in the 1870's brought an end to the era of the wild buffalo (bison), which had been the staff of life to the Plains Indians and the main food supply on the white man's frontier. A small captive herd of bison is preserved today in nearby Wildcat Hills State Park. The bighorn and the grizzly, described by early travelers, disappeared by 1860, leaving an occasional rare skull as their last testament. The pronghorn (antelope) is still common in the tablelands north and south of Scotts Bluff, but deer are the only large hoofed animals which still frequent the monument area. Other survivors include red fox, coyote, raccoon, porcupine, badger, beaver, muskrat, and fox squirrel. Prairie dogs, once abundant, have virtually disappeared.

There is a wide variety of bird life. Some of the species that have been seen at Scotts Bluff are—double-crested cormorant, great blue heron, black-crowned night heron, mallard, green-winged and blue-winged teal, American merganser, turkey vulture, red-tailed hawk, golden eagle, sparrow hawk, killdeer, spotted sandpiper, Franklin's gull, mourning dove, great horned owl, (western) burrowing owl,

Mule Deer are often seen by park visitors.

western kingbird, horned lark, cliff swallow, American magpie, rock wren, mockingbird, mountain bluebird, Townsend's solitaire, loggerhead shrike, western meadowlark, and spotted towhee junco.

Prehistory of the Scotts Bluff Region

Although collections of stone projectile points, scrapers, hammerstones, knives, clay pottery, and other primitive Indian artifacts have been assembled from scattered sites in the North Platte Valley, the story of prehistoric man in the Scotts Bluff region is still incomplete. Only a dim outline of the ancient past is beginning to emerge from the patient studies of archeologists.

Vague evidence of aboriginal campsites and signal fires has been found on the summit of Scotts Bluff. However, the story of ancient man in this section of the Great Plains is better suggested by five other nearby Indian occupation sites:

Signal Butte. At the western terminus of Wildcat Hills, about 12 miles southwest of Scotts Bluff, archeologists of Nebraska University, in 1932, probed the top of an isolated bluff which is now famous as a key archeological site. A 13-foot vertical cross section revealed three separate levels, each bearing cultural material. The lowest level is believed to represent a hunting complex (Early Lithic Period), perhaps 5,000 years old. The second level (Intermediate Lithic Period), described as Pre-Woodland, is given a tentative age of 1,500 years. The uppermost level (Ceramic Period) contains artifacts of the Dismal River and Upper Republican cultures, including pottery. The primitive farmers representing the Upper Republican culture occupied Signal Butte when Columbus discovered America, while the Dismal River people believed to have been an Apache group of about A. D. 1700.

Scotts Bluff Bison Quarry. In 1933 archeologists of the University of Nebraska State Museum, while excavating in the bank of Kiowa Creek, near Signal Butte, found stone projectile points in association with an extinct form of giant bison. This remarkable find, which established Scottsbluff points as a classic type, was among the earliest of a series of discoveries in the Great Plains which have furnished unmistakable evidence of mysterious big game hunters who inhabited the Plains some 10,000 years ago.

Spanish Diggings. About 60 miles northwest of Scotts Bluff, in Wyoming, lies an extensive area of flinty hills and wastes which have large numbers of ancient quarries. Thousands of artifacts of primitive manufacture suggest the Intermediate Lithic Period preceding the dawn of the Christian era.

Scotts Bluff Potato Cellar Site. Near the east slope of Scotts Bluff,

Yucca in bloom at the summit of Scotts Bluff.

in 1934, a farmer reported the occurrence of several skeletons and associated stone and bone artifacts while excavating for a potato storage bin. This appears to have been a burial ground of early Nebraska hunters, or foragers, possibly contemporary with the Intermediate Lithic level at Signal Butte.

Ash Hollow Cave. About 100 miles downstream from Scotts Bluff, near a famous Oregon Trail campsite, is a rock shelter, excavated by the Nebraska State Historical Society in 1939, which contained evidence of 7 occupations over a period of 2,000 years. These range from the Intermediate Lithic, or second level at Signal Butte, through the Woodland, Upper Republican, and Dismal River complexes of the Ceramic Period.

When white men first penetrated Nebraska, about A. D. 1700, the Central Plains were divided into hunting areas held by tribes living in large fortified villages. They fed on buffalo meat obtained by seasonal hunts, and on corn, beans, and squash grown near their villages. The Pawnee were the dominant Nebraska tribe when the region was first seen by white men, but the region was soon invaded by Sioux, Cheyenne, Kiowa, and other tribes. With the introduction of horses and guns by Europeans, the Plains Indians became the bold, wide-ranging buffalo hunters and fighters famous in annals of the white man's Wild West.

Guide to the Area

Location of the Monument. Scotts Bluff National Monument adjoins the south bank of the North Platte River, in Scotts Bluff County, western Nebraska, 3 miles west of Gering via State Route 92, and 4 miles southwest of Scottsbluff which is on the north side of the river, on U. S. 26. The highway route on the north side of the North Platte River from Broadwater to the city of Scottsbluff in part parallels the course of the Mormon Trail. If you approach this historic landmark from the east, you can follow the classic Oregon Trail route to this point by driving up the North Platte Valley via U. S. 26 from Ogallala through Bridgeport (Courthouse Rock) to South Bayard (Chimney Rock) and State Route 92 from South Bayard to Gering.

Trans-Monument Road. The monument area is bisected from east to west by State Route 92, the principal approach being from the east through Gering. The Mitchell Pass route of the old Oregon Trail coming in from the east to the north of Dome Rock intersects this highway just south of the east entrance to Scotts Bluff National Monument. From this entrance to monument headquarters, the highway roughly follows the roadbed of the old Oregon Trail. Near monument headquarters, remains of the trail swing south of the highway before recrossing it to make the ascent through Mitchell Pass, which separates South Bluff from Scotts Bluff proper.

Mitchell Pass Area. At the crest of Mitchell Pass, State Route 92 continues westward through Mitchell Valley to the Wyoming State line. From the pass, the trough of the Oregon Trail makes an abrupt hairpin turn around the head of a ravine, then veers northward toward the North Platte River and the old crossing at the mouth of Horse Creek, near Lyman, Nebraska. In Mitchell Pass and for a few hundred yards west of the museum, the Oregon Trail trough is exceptionally well-defined, despite the passage of over 100 years since it was heavily traveled. The unusual depth of the old trail through this area is a result of the countless thousands of animals and wagons that had to pass single file through the Mitchell Pass bottleneck. A trail from the Mitchell Pass parking area leads to where William H. Jackson camped in 1866.

Visitor Center. The dominant building at the monument headquarters area, just east of Mitchell Pass, is the visitor center, which houses the Oregon Trail Museum and monument administrative offices. The museum exhibits feature the Oregon Trail and the emigrants who used it, geological formations, early Indian inhabitants of the Scotts Bluff area, and the works of William Henry Jackson, artist-photographer.

Uniformed personnel are stationed at the visitor center throughout the year. A schedule of seasonal public services, including an orientation program, walks, talks, living history demonstrations, and evening programs throughout the summer months, is available at the visitor center.

Scotts Bluff Summit Road and Summit Area. During the 1930s, a paved road 1.7 miles in length, requiring three tunnel excavations, was built from the headquarters area to the summit to enhance visitor appreciation of the bluff's scenic and historic values. The road leads to a 50-car parking area on top. At the Summit Road entrance gate, adjoining the visitor center, cars are welcomed by a uniformed ranger. There is a fee collected here for use of the Summit Road, which is open daily except when weather conditions make driving hazardous.

The summit area covers several acres. Surfaced trails reach the principal overlooks. The main trail proceeds north from the area to the High Point of the bluff (4,649 feet above sea level), then meanders to the Observation Point above the north face of the bluff. At the foot of the bluff are the scenic badlands and the North Platte River, while the historic North Platte Valley stretches to the horizon east and west. Exhibits along the summit trail tell about the Oregon Trail and the geological formations of Scotts Bluff.

A trail south from the parking area will enable you to reach a point overlooking the Visitor Center, Mitchell Pass, and the beginning loop of the Summit Road. Beyond Dome Rock is Gering Valley, through which was the Robidoux Pass route of the Oregon Trail.

Saddle Rock Trail. A feature of the monument which affords extra scenic and inspirational benefit is a 1.6-mile-long trail extending from the summit to the headquarters area via a series of zig-zags and ledges, a foot tunnel, and "Scott's Spring." Not only does this trail afford superb scenic views of the bluff, it enables you to examine at close hand the successive rock strata that comprise the bluff, and to walk through varyingly vegetated slopes and fields. Descent of the bluff on foot by this trail is a popular activity. There are those who arrange to have someone in their party drive the car back down to the headquarters area, while others make the round trip by foot.

Badlands Area. The section between the steep bluff and the river is characterized by a tortuous labyrinth of steep-sided gullies known as "badlands." The badlands area is of historical interest since it was the impassability of this ground that forced the earliest emigrants on the trail to detour away from the river, first through Robidoux Pass, and later through Mitchell Pass. The badlands are also of exceptional geologic interest as an example of rapid erosion in soft rock beds of comparatively uniform composition.

Visitors on the Oregon Trail west of Mitchell Pass.

Off-Trail Use. The area within the monument has few modern improvements. It is relatively unspoiled, with considerable scenic, geological, and botanical features. You are free to hike throughout the park, but no fires or camping are permitted. Because of the rugged terrain, rough clothing and stout footgear are recommended. Climbing within the monument is discouraged due to the unstable and historic nature of the sandstone cliffs.

Related Areas

There are several other areas administered by or affiliated with the National Park Service that commemorate phases of Oregon Trail history. These include: Jefferson National Expansion Memorial in Missouri, Chimney Rock National Historic Site and Homestead National Monument in Nebraska, Fort Laramie National Historic Site in Wyoming, McLoughlin House National Historic Site in Oregon, and Fort Vancouver National Historic Site and Whitman Mission National Historic Site in Washington. Oregon National Historic Trail traces the main route west for the early emigrants.

Administration

Scotts Bluff National Monument was set aside by presidential proclamation on December 12, 1919. The park contains approximately 3,000 acres of high sandstone bluffs and prairie habitat. For information contact: Superintendent, Scotts Bluff NM, P.O. Box 27, Gering, NE 69341.

Suggested Readings

CHITTENDEN, HIRAM M., *American Fur Trade of the Far West.* 2 vols. Rufus Rockwell Wilson, Inc., New York, 1936.

DRIGGS, HOWARD R., *Westward America* (with reproductions of water-color paintings by William H. Jackson). Somerset Books, Inc., New York, 1942.

FEDERAL WRITERS' PROJECT, *The Oregon Trail.* Hastings House, New York, 1939.

GHENT, W. J., *The Road to Oregon.* Longmans, Green and Co., New York, 1929.

HULBERT, ARCHER B., *Forty-Niners, the Chronicle of the California Trail.* Blue Ribbon Books, Inc., New York, 1931.

JACKSON, JOSEPH H., ed., *Gold Rush Album.* Charles Scribner's Sons, New York, 1949.

LAVENDER, DAVID, *The Overland Migrations.* National Park Service, Washington, D.C., 1980.

MATTES, MERRILL J., *The Great Platte River Road.* Nebraska State Historical Society, Lincoln, 1969.

MONAGHAN, JAY, *The Overland Trail.* The Bobbs-Merrill Co., Indianapolis, 1947.

OLSON, JAMES C., *History of Nebraska.* University of Nebraska Press, Lincoln, 1955.

PADEN, IRENE D., *The Wake of the Prairie Schooner.* The MacMillan Co., New York, 1943.

PARKMAN, FRANCIS, *The Oregon Trail.* Langhart and Co., Inc., New York, 1931.

ROLLINS, PHILLIP A., ed., *Discovery of the Oregon Trail: Robert Stuart's Narratives.* Edward Eberstadt and Sons, New York, 1935.

UNRUH, JOHN D. JR., *The Plains Across.* University of Illinois Press, Chicago, 1979.

U.S. GOVERNMENT PRINTING OFFICE: 1995-0-401-376